God Answers
Prayers

Allison Bottke
with **Cheryll Hutchings**

Dee —
May God always answer your prayer
Alli Bottke

HARVEST HOUSE PUBLISHERS

EUGENE, OREGON

To protect the privacy of the individuals involved in the following stories, the names have been changed when deemed appropriate.

Cover by Left Coast Design, Portland, Oregon

GOD ANSWERS PRAYERS
Copyright © 2005 by Allison Bottke
Published by Harvest House Publishers
Eugene, Oregon 97402
www.harvesthousepublishers.com

Library of Congress Cataloging-in-Publication Data
Bottke, Allison.
    God answers prayers / Allison Bottke with Cheryll Hutchings.
        p. cm. — (God answers prayers)
    ISBN 0-7369-1587-7 (pbk.)
    1. Prayer—Christianity.   I. Hutchings, Cheryll.   II. Title.   III. Series.
    BV220.B66 2005
    242—dc22   2004026526

Printed in the United States of America
05   06   07   08   09   10   11   12   /   VP-MS   /   10   9   8   7   6   5   4   3   2   1

To my husband, Kevin Bottke.
God answered my prayer when
He brought us together.
I love you.

and…

To Jim and Janice Chaffee.
May God
bring you peace
of mind and heart
and answers to
your prayers.

Contents

Foreword by Lowell Lundstrom 9

Acknowledgments 10

A Note from Allison 11

1. The Wisdom of Children 13
   "Beulah's Bull Calf" by Candy Abbott 14
   "A Life Saved" by Iris Gray Dowling 18
   "Roy, Trigger, and God" by Rev. Michael Welmer 21
   "Kassie's Kittens" by Lou Killian Zywicki 23
   "One Child's Prayer" by Deanna Luke 26
   "Coco Comes Home" by Ann Oliver 29

2. God's Divine Protection 31
   "A Night of Peril" by Susan M. Foster (as told by
      Richard Anderson) 32
   "Cliff-hanger" by Clement Hanson 36
   "Angels Watching over Little Nancy" by Gloria
      Cassity Stargel (as told by Sue Jones) 40

3. All Creatures Great and Small 47
   "Do You Trust Me?" by Wendy Dellinger 48
   "Life Is Precious Where There Is Love" by
      Joan Clayton 52
   "Angel with an Attitude" by Susan Farr Fahncke 55
   "Sunday School Lesson on the Front Porch" by
      Cheryl Scott Norwood 58

4. God's Strength in Our Weakness 61
   "Bull Attack" by Kevin Bottke 63
   "Strangers No More" by Delores Christian Liesner 69

"My Wife's Answered Prayer" by Emory G. May   73

"The Rest of the Story" by T. Suzanne Eller   76

"Not Impossible with God" by P. Jeanne Davis   80

5. God at the Hour of Death   85

"With Sighs Too Deep for Words" by
Michael Dandridge   86

"Hands Around the Bed" by Sharon M. Knudson   92

"God Is Good...All the Time" by Jan Roadarmel Ledford
(as told by Herman Parramore)   95

"No Is an Answer" by June L. Varnum   99

"The Prayer" by Roger Allen Cook   103

"Heaven in My Dreams" by Andrea Boeshaar   106

6. A Change of Heart   111

"Fireplug No More" by Rusty Fischer   112

"A Day of Miracles" by Bob Haslam   117

"POW" by Anne Johnson   121

"My Precious Prodigal" by Lowell Lundstrom   124

"A New Heart" by Barbara E. Haley   130

"A Marriage Made in Heaven" by Thelma Wells   133

7. Finding Love   137

"All Things for the Good" by Dennis Van Scoy Sr.   138

"A Mission of Love" by Sharon L. Fawcett   142

"The Healing Power of Forgiveness" by
Karen O'Connor   147

"For Better or Worse...with Boxing Gloves and
Running Shoes" by Jennifer S. McMahan   151

"What Does Anna Need?" by Sandra McGarrity   155

8. God and the "Little Things" in Life 159

   "Dance for Me" by B. J. Jensen 160

   "God and the Map" by Suzan Strader 165

   "Be Still with God" by Nancy B. Gibbs 167

9. On Foreign Soil 171

   "The Voice of God" by Renie Szilak Burghardt 172

   "Miracle Behind the Iron Curtain" by Bob Kelly 176

   "Missionary Miracle" by Sharon Hinck 178

   "Drive-by Blessing" by Susanna Flory 183

   "Simple Faith" by Muriel Larson 185

10. The Prayers God Always Says Yes To 189

   "The Day the Cheering Stopped" by Gloria Cassity Stargel
     (as told by John C. Stewart) 191

   "Get on Your Knees When You Don't Know What
     to Do" by Phyllis Wallace 195

   "A Nurse's Prayer" by Penelope Carlevato 197

   "Meeting in a Snowbank" by Dr. Tom C. Rakow 200

   "Answered Prayer-on-a-Stick" by Sandra Snider 202

   "No Small Miracle" by R. T. Byrum 205

   "Getting Lost, Getting Home" by Nan McKenzie
     Kosowan 209

    About the Contributors to *God Answers Prayers* 211

    10 Tips on How To Pray 219

Foreword

Are you facing an impossible situation and need a miracle?

Consider the words of Jesus in these two verses of Scripture: "All things are possible with God" (Mark 10:27). "You may ask me for anything in my name, and I will do it" (John 14:14).

Prayer has unlimited possibilities for it releases the power of God on your behalf. Everything is possible with God. Requests, presented to God in the powerful name of Jesus, are answered.

But the doubts that roam around our subconscious minds challenge us, saying, "Prove it!"

Our response should be a bold and emphatic *"Read this!"* As we read what God has done for other people, our own faith is kindled and our doubts overcome.

After the crucifixion, two disciples of Jesus were walking down the Emmaus Road when a stranger appeared and began to walk with them, inquiring about the events that had shaken the city. *It was Jesus in disguise.*

The Bible says in Luke 24:27, "And beginning with Moses and all the Prophets, he explained to them what was said in all the Scriptures concerning himself." Later that evening, when they sat down to eat, their eyes were opened and they realized this stranger was Jesus. Then they said, "Were not our hearts burning within us while he talked with us on the road and opened the Scriptures to us?" (Luke 24:32).

As they heard the great stories of faith and of God's deliverance, they experienced a holy heartburn. Suddenly the cloud of doubt lifted, and the light of truth ignited their hearts. They understood why Jesus had to die and be raised again from the dead.

These stories, compiled like the famous "Chicken Soup for the Soul" series, will light a fire of faith in your heart. Read a couple of the stories every day. God loves you more than you will ever know, and He will open your spiritual eyes to the truth in the confusion around you.

Allison Bottke and her team of editors have chosen the best stories to bless you and help you through your trials.

Two things are needed for a miracle: 1. An impossibility, and 2. God's intervention.

Be encouraged. If you are facing an impossible situation, you are halfway to a miracle.

—Lowell Lundstrom

Acknowledgments

Special blessings to our editorial team: Susan Fahncke, Cheryll Hutchings, Terri McPherson, and Sharen Watson.

God has often answered my prayers by bringing special people into my life—people who love and support me, pray with and for me, make me laugh and cry, and hold me accountable.

While there is no way I could possibly thank everyone who made this book possible, I would like to extend warm, appreciative hugs to the following folks:

All of our contributing authors, God bless you!

And to Marlene Bagnull, the Bird Family, Penny Carlevato, Jennifer Cary, Victor and Dorothy Constien, Lisa Copen, Mickey Crippen, Eva Marie Everson, Pam Farrell, Greg and Cathie Gappa, Heather Gemmen, Michelle McKinney Hammond, Nick Harrison, Cory Howard, Anne Johnson, LaRose Karr, Gene and Carol Kent, Ken and Loretta Knight, Linda Lagnada, Jocelyn Lansing, Steve Laube, Florence Littauer, Marita Littauer, Don and Gladys Longpre, Lowell and Connie Lundstrom, Chip MacGregor, Carolyn McCourtney, Carolyn McCready, Mary McNeal, Dale Meyer, Diane O'Brian, Stormie Omartian, Susan Titus Osborn, Tracie Peterson, Marilyn Phillips, Linda Evans Shepherd, Betty Southard, Tammy Thorpe, Brad and Mary Utpadel, Thelma Wells, Sandra Wenker, Pamela Wetzell, and Terry Whalin.

And to my AWSA sisters, my CLASS family, the Masterpiece Studios crew, my Writers View sisters and brothers, and last but no means least, the very special God Allows U-Turns prayer team.

And to my children Christopher Smith, Mandy Bottke, Kermit and Jennifer Bottke, and Kyle Bottke. My prayer is for your prayers to be answered. I love you.

A Note from Allison

I believe in prayer—at least I do now.

Let me tell you my story, and I think you will see why.

My parents divorced when I was young, leaving an emptiness in my heart I could never understand. As a teenager, I felt apart from girls my own age, and I rebelled strongly against authority. I had given up on God long before I ran away at the age of 15 to marry the 18-year-old man who in one year went from being the love of my life to my abuser, jailer, kidnapper, rapist, and attempted murderer. By the time I was "Sweet 16," there was no doubt in my mind: If God existed, it was certainly not in my world.

After the birth of my son and my divorce, both at the age of 16, there was no room in my life for anything but the here and now. Practical things consumed me, like going back to school, working, child care, housekeeping, paying bills, and learning how to be a mother. I filled my days with busy, take-charge tasks. I filled my nights with alcohol, drugs, parties, and self-destruction. I filled my soul with empty promises and emptier pursuits. I was lost.

Why did it seem as though nothing I did worked out? Why did I feel so worthless? The feelings of utter helplessness and hopelessness, of unrealized dreams, broken promises, and dead-end streets overwhelmed me.

One summer evening I was taking a walk in my neighborhood when I noticed people going into a local church. Suddenly my legs developed a mind of their own, virtually propelling me up the steps and through the doors.

Alone in the church balcony, I looked toward the pulpit and saw the statue of Jesus with outstretched hands, looking right at me. Hot tears fell down my cheeks as emotions I could not explain filled my heart and soul.

What was wrong? What was happening to me? Why was I sitting in a strange church and crying like a baby? When the pastor began to speak, his message was for me. It was a message of being lost, without direction, without hope, without faith—and how that could be changed. He talked of how we needed only to listen to the Holy Spirit and ask the Lord Jesus Christ to come into our heart and He would be there—just like that.

Suddenly, I wanted to know more about this relationship with Jesus of which the pastor spoke.

And so I *prayed,* asking God to turn me around, to set me on a new course. He said yes, and my walk with the Lord started that day—a day that forever changed my life. I was 35 years old.

As a result of that prayer and the many prayers since that day, the world opened up to me in ways I could never have imagined. Opportunities, experiences, and spiritual illumination did not suddenly make everything perfect, but my life became one of healing and hope, a life of promise where before there had been empty desolation. I had made a U-turn, and my life journey now had purpose.

I did not "get religion." I made a spiritual connection with God as a result of prayer that turned my life around. I "got a relationship"—a relationship with Jesus Christ, and my life has never been the same.

Prayer works! God hears! We have only to ask and to believe. May God use the following stories of answered prayer to encourage you in your faith in Him.

1
The Wisdom of Children

Innocent, poignant, and often impractical, children's prayers touch our hearts and God's. Yet the requests of these precious little ones seem to bring about the impossible. Matthew 18:10 reminds us that their angels continually behold God's face. Should we be surprised then when we see how God responds to the faith of a child?

Though we are the ones instructed to teach them in the ways of the Lord, we would do well to learn from them about simple trust in our Maker.

O Lord, may our faith always be pure, innocent, trusting, and childlike.

> *Let the little children come to me, and do not hinder them, for the kingdom of God belongs to such as these. I tell you the truth, anyone who will not receive the kingdom of God like a little child will never enter it* (Mark 10:14-15).

Children can teach all of us great lessons, especially in the area of answered prayer. Candy, Mike, and Jimmy knew this and prayed to the Lord to help them. Who else would take the time to save a little ole beef cow?

Beulah's Bull Calf

BY CANDY ABBOTT, GEORGETOWN, DELAWARE

"Mike, Jimmy, come quick!" I yelled through their bedroom door. "Dad says Beulah's having her calf right now!"

It was 1957, and I was ten years old. The smell of straw filled our nostrils as we scurried to our makeshift barn. The shed where we usually kept our tractor was now home to Beulah, the borrowed cow, and her newborn.

"Come take a look." Dad spoke quietly, directing us to join him on the other side of Beulah. There he was: the ugliest, most wonderful hodgepodge of lanky legs, knobby knees, and slimy body I had ever seen. Beulah, an attentive mother, was licking her calf, cleaning him lovingly.

"Yuck!" My brother Jimmy made a sour face while taking in the sight.

"It's not yucky," I said. "All babies are born with that stuff on them, and all animal mommies clean it off by licking. It's like giving their babies kisses."

"Is it a boy cow or a girl cow?" Mike asked.

"A boy calf isn't a cow," Dad explained. "It's a bull. And this is a bull calf."

"A bull calf!" Mike and Jimmy hopped around like kangaroos on a trampoline. "What are we going to name him?"

"Calm down, boys. We're not going to name this calf." Dad's expression changed to one of serious concern.

"Dad, why not?" I asked. "We always name our animals."

"Not this time, honey." He stopped rubbing Beulah, put the towel down, and knelt beside us. "Remember, Beulah isn't really our cow. We just let her stay here for a friend. In exchange, we get to keep the milk. Your mom fixes it to make butter and cream for our family."

He went on to explain that part of the bargain also included a promise that when the calf grew to 80 pounds, Dad could take him to be butchered for veal so our family could eat. Mirroring his sad expression, we didn't really understand what he was saying.

As soon as our talk was over, my brothers and I tiptoed over to the calf. We secretly vowed to think up a good name for him.

Seven days a week, when the rooster crowed at sunrise, Dad would pull on his khaki pants and work boots and make his way to our backyard barn. The no-name calf grew stronger and larger every day, even as I secretly prayed he would stay small.

Every day as Dad stirred the mixture of ground corn and bran for Beulah, the bull calf would rub against his thigh. And each time he milked Beulah, the calf would nose around for attention.

One afternoon I overheard Dad tell Mom, "It's like that calf thinks I'm his mother."

I noticed that he would pat the calf on the head every now and then. But he still wouldn't let us name him.

"Mike. Jimmy." I pulled my younger brothers close. "I've got a good name for the bull calf. What do you think of 'Nosey'?"

They let out a quiet cheer and, from that moment on, Nosey became our secret pet.

Eventually, Dad taught me to milk Beulah, and I took over the duty on Saturday mornings while Dad was plowing. Mike and Jimmy liked to watch me.

"Can I try?" Mike asked.

"Sure," I said, feeling very grown-up. "But you have to watch out for her hind legs so she doesn't kick by mistake."

Jimmy entertained Nosey while Mike got into position, cautiously making his way around the towering cow. He perched proudly on the wooden, three-legged stool. Just as Dad had taught me, I leaned over and placed my hands around Mike's small fingers, demonstrating how to grip, pull, and aim for the bucket.

"Ow!" Mike gasped, as the warm milk sprayed in his hand. "It's hot."

"It's not hot." It seemed my brother expected the milk to come out cold, like it comes out of the refrigerator. I laughed at the thought.

All too soon, the day came when the calf weighed 80 pounds. Dad announced, with a crack in his voice, "I guess it's time to load the bull calf up."

"What do you mean, Daddy?" I still didn't quite understand where he was taking Nosey.

"As much as I hate to do it, kids, I have to take the calf to the Townsend Slaughter House."

"What's a slaughterhouse?"

"It's a place where they butcher livestock and wrap it to order. They have a meat locker and freezer, and they take care of everything right there."

I still didn't understand.

As tenderly as he could, Dad explained what he was going to do. "Remember when the calf was born and I told you when he got big enough I'd have to butcher him for veal? That means we have to kill the calf so we'll have meat for the winter."

"No!" I screamed and ran out of the room. "I'll never eat meat again!"

I watched from my bedroom window as Dad walked resolutely, but with slumped shoulders, into the backyard and unlatched the barn door. He wiped his cheek with the back of his hand. Our calf innocently followed him outside and stood meekly beside our '48 Dodge Town and Country. I watched as Dad took out the backseat and folded down the middle one. He lifted Nosey's front legs, gave him a pat on the rear and, like a child eager for a ride, the calf jumped over the tailgate. The grate of the metal as Dad slammed the door echoed in my ears like a deathblow.

I turned away, unable to watch him drive off. Mom came in to try and comfort me, but I waved her away. How could she let Dad do this?

"Dear God," I prayed, "please don't let Nosey get butchered. Oh please, do something to bring him back to us." I had prayed a lot as a kid, but this was the first time I offered so earnest a prayer. All three of us kids prayed hard that day.

A half an hour later, much sooner than expected, I heard the familiar sound of the station wagon engine and crunch of tires in our driveway.

"He's back!" Mike yelled. "Nosey's back!" Jimmy bounded into my room, grinning and jumping up and down. "Come and see!"

Sure enough, gangly legs and hooves clambered their way over the station wagon tailgate, landing unsteadily and kicking up a small cloud of dust in the driveway. As Dad led Nosey back to the barn to reunite with his mother, the three of us hugged our bull calf's neck and patted his silky ears. "What happened? What's he doing back here?"

We couldn't tell if Dad was crying or laughing as he choked out his explanation. "The whole way into town, he kept rubbing his wet nose against my neck. I'd shoo him back, and the next thing I knew, he's slobbering wet kisses all over my face with that soft, fat tongue of his. I kept thinking, "This is wrong. You can't do this, Jack. As much as you don't want to admit it, he's a family pet. You don't take pets to the butcher. So I turned around, and here we are. What do you say we give this pet a name?"

"Dad," I giggled, looking at my brothers' excited faces, "we have a confession to make. We named him a long time ago. We call him Nosey!"

"Obviously the perfect name, since it was his wet nose on my neck that made me change my mind and bring him home." Dad reached down to pat our bull calf and chuckled.

My brothers and I learned a lot that day. It was a time when our faith became grounded in the power of prayer. We learned that daddies can change their minds, that daddies hear the heart cry of their children, and that daddies have feelings, too.

We also learned that our Abba Daddy, our Father, answers prayer. Sometimes Daddy God says no, like keeping Nosey less than 80 pounds, because sometimes He has a better plan. And sometimes He says yes, and brings him home.

Nosey grew up to be a fat, sassy bull that won several 4-H ribbons at the state fair. He taught us far more in his lifetime than we would ever have imagined: lessons like responsibility, dependability, pride, commitment, and love.

Forty-three years later, I can still see Nosey's furry face in my mind's eye, and he's smiling, thankful for the full life he lived as a result of prayer.

Teaching our children to pray, especially in times of need, is a necessity. With acts of pure evil being committed every day, we must arm them with the power of prayer. Irene used that power during a frightful time that could have changed the course of her life, and Iris knew the Lord had answered her.

A Life Saved

by Iris Gray Dowling, Cochranville, Pennsylvania

"Help, help!" The shrill voice was coming from the grassy meadow between my house and the road.

I had just sent my daughter to the bus stop and climbed back into bed. Sick that day, I had called in to work and told them I wouldn't be in.

"Help!" I heard the voice again. Jumping out of bed, I wrapped my robe around me and grabbed my old coat.

"Please, God, please let my daughter arrive safely at school." I heard an engine take off near the bus stop.

Again, I heard faint cries coming from the pasture. Heart pumping, I raced toward the sound, but could only see tall grass. As I got closer to the crying, I recognized a young girl struggling toward me. Irene, a friend of my daughter, was out of breath and terrified. She should have already been picked up. Her bus stop was just before my daughter's, a mile away on the other side of some wooded hills.

"Help me! Please, help me!" she panted.

I rushed to her side, and out of the corner of my eye noticed someone running to a car parked near the bridge, about an eighth of a mile across the meadow. The car turned onto the road and headed toward my daughter's bus stop.

I didn't think about my daughter being in imminent danger. I was pretty sure that I had heard the bus pull away. My immediate concern was this exhausted little girl. I reached out and took her hand, helping her stand up. I wrapped her in my coat and held her close as we walked slowly to my house.

"What were you doing out in the pasture on such a cold morning, honey? Did you lose one of your pets?"

"I w...w-was waiting for the bus, and a car stopped. The man told me to get in the car because my mom sent him to take me to her office. I said no and tried to run away." Irene broke into tears. "He got out of the car and grabbed me. He stuffed me in the car and locked the doors. He was going so fast."

"Irene, have you ever seen this man before?"

"No, and I didn't look at him very much. I was just trying to figure a way to get out of the car. The door locks looked like the ones in my mom and dad's car, and when he slowed down for an oncoming car at the one-lane bridge, I unlocked the door and jumped into the ditch. I got up and squeezed through the post and the fence rail, crossed the swamp, and ran as fast as I could up the hill to your house." Irene breathed deeply, finally catching her breath. "He wouldn't give up, though. He chased me. I prayed and prayed that you were home."

"Any other day, I wouldn't have been here. God answered your prayers today, Irene." I offered her some warm tea. A little calmer now, she remembered her mother's work number, and I called to let Mrs. Mac know that Irene was safe with me until she could make her way home.

Suddenly my thoughts shifted to my own daughter. Did she really get on the bus? I called the school. I waited and prayed until they assured me my daughter was safe in her classroom.

At the end of the school day, police came to question us about our experience and observations. "I remember a light-blue car stopping near the bus stop after I was already on the bus. It followed us for a little while," my daughter offered.

I told them everything I could think of. Later that day, while watching the news broadcast, I learned that a serial rapist had been in our area that day. He had tried to pick up several other girls without success.

When I saw Irene again, I told her that God had indeed answered her prayer that day. "Several miracles saved your life, Irene. On any other day, I would have been on my way to work. I very rarely take a sick day." I also explained that another car was in just the right place, obstructing her abductor from taking the one-lane bridge too quickly, offering her the opportunity to escape. "Irene, God also gave you the wisdom to see that option. He gave you strength to get through the swamp and up the steep hill to my house."

God had answered my prayers, too. My daughter arrived safely to school. Even though we didn't know the extent of our danger that morning, none of us has forgotten this experience. We are strengthened in our belief and our trust in God's answers to prayer.

What a blessing to experience the true power of prayer, especially as a child. Can you remember the very first time you prayed and were astonished at how quickly and easily God answered that prayer? Michael was only six or seven at the time (he cannot quite remember what his age was), but he can definitely remember the prayer, and it changed the way he viewed prayer for the rest of his life.

Roy, Trigger, and God

BY REV. MICHAEL WELMER, HOUSTON, TEXAS

At one time or another, each of us experiences an omnipotent moment. It is the click of the clock when a prayer for something so seemingly impossible is answered by the almighty power of God. An omnipotent moment can fortify the foundation of our faith for all our future days when we are called upon to rely on the promises of God.

My omnipotent moment occurred when I was about six or seven years old. Roy Rogers, the "King of the Cowboys," was on a promotional tour for Sears and Roebuck. One Saturday morning, Roy and Trigger were scheduled to be at the Sears store in downtown Indianapolis where my dad was the store superintendent. I dressed in my Roy Rogers finest. I strapped on my Roy Rogers gun belt, donned my Roy Rogers boots, and tipped my cowboy hat in just the right direction. I was ready to meet my hero.

Everyone gathered on the loading dock to hear Roy speak to us about obeying our parents, being kind to others, and eating healthy. Roy and Trigger did a few tricks, and then Roy made a special announcement. "As a special award for being good, one little girl or boy will get to sit on Trigger." Roy carefully scanned the crowd of children.

"Please, God, let him choose me! Please, please, God. Let me be the one who gets to sit on Trigger! Oh, God, I will never ask for anything else, if You can get him to pick me. Please, God, please." I tried my best to sit as still as I could, with perfect posture and my hands crossed in my lap.

The next moment is etched in my memory forever. I watched Roy Rogers walk from child to child, and when he got to me, he stopped.

"How about you, young man? Would you like to be the buckaroo to sit on my horse, Trigger?"

"Would I!" The "King of the Cowboys" lifted me up in his arms and sat me on Trigger. God had answered my prayer, and I was on top of the world, looking down from the back of my hero's horse.

This was my omnipotent moment. It was such a powerful experience, that it molded my faith to believe that nothing was too hard for the Lord.

"Is anything too hard for the Lord?" Certainly, those words pave the way for God's children to "cast all their cares upon Him." As the disciples witnessed the incarnation of those words in the very miracle of Jesus, and ultimately in His resurrection, they each discovered their own omnipotent moments, moving them to a greater reliance on God's almighty power.

My story of Roy and Trigger and the omnipotence of God is not finished yet. My dad was most certainly the person responsible for arranging Roy and Trigger's visit to Sears, and though I never asked him, I believe that he somehow "encouraged" Roy to pick me up. How he did it, I don't know. I may never know, but I would have done the same for my son.

Yet, it really doesn't matter if my dad did "encourage" Roy to choose me. Isn't that how God works to construct His omnipotent moments? He acts through the people around us to create our omnipotent moments and works through us to craft the omnipotent moments of others. Sometimes that is called answered prayer.

It doesn't matter how God did it, who He used to do it, or what circumstances He marshaled to make it happen. All that mattered for me, and that which still shapes my prayer life, is this: If God could put me on Trigger, He can do anything!

During times of life's disappointments and changes, even small matters can seem insurmountable obstacles. Kassie knew what she wanted and asked God to deliver. Like most parents, Kassie's mom could not see how this special prayer could make a difference. God showed her how.

Kassie's Kittens

BY LOU KILLIAN ZYWICKI, CLANTON, MINNESOTA

As I looked around our four-room apartment I was repulsed. It hadn't been updated in 50 years. There was gray paint on top of years of spongy wallpaper, the varnish was worn off the kitchen cabinets, and the linoleum on the kitchen floor was so badly cracked that it was hard to scrub it. After years of being college rental property, the smell of beer and stale cigarettes was so deeply embedded that the gallons of Lysol I had scoured into everything still had not removed the odor.

Worst of all, our three youngest children and our beagle shared one bedroom. We had squeezed two sets of bunk beds into the bedroom, and these were occupied by our 15-year-old daughter, Karin, our 12-year-old son, Kendal, and our 6-year-old daughter, Kassie. Luckily, Kris, our oldest, had already moved away from home, or we would have been even more crowded. The children gained privacy by changing clothes in the bathroom, and our daughter Karin did her nightly studying at the city library, but none of us were dealing very well with our new living situation.

Our family business had failed, leaving us deeply in debt, and we had few options. We had to sell the lovely home that we had spent the past nine years remodeling. My husband and I each had new jobs, and we knew that we would slowly climb out of our financial hole, but for now we were living in an old apartment building that we were renovating.

My deepest concern was for my daughter Kassie. We had adopted her when she was four. Her early years had been very difficult and had left her traumatized. Now, just when she was beginning to do better, we had moved into this ugly, crowded living space. Each member of our family was grieving individual losses, and tempers were short. I knew Kassie didn't need this added stress.

Kassie had her own cure for the sadness she felt. She decided she needed a kitten to snuggle and love. She stubbornly refused to listen when I tried to explain that we just didn't have room for another pet. Instead, each night when she knelt to say her prayers, she asked God to send her a kitty. I knew that her solution was not the correct one, but I did not know what to do. I, too, prayed for an answer that would make our living conditions a little happier.

One evening I sat on the edge of Kassie's bed absently stroking her soft, red hair as she engaged in her daily discussion with God. My heart ached with her longing and with my own unhappiness. After tucking her tightly into her bunk, I went to find a box of Kassie's winter clothing that I had stored in the garage and found an unwelcome surprise waiting for me in the box. A mama cat had made her bed there, and she lay nursing two tiny gray kittens.

I refused to admit that Kassie's prayer had been answered and told no one about the kittens' presence. But on Halloween night we had an intense blizzard, and for some unknown reason the mama cat disappeared into the storm. I did not have a choice. I had to bring the kittens into the house and bottle-feed them, or leave them in the garage to die.

When she spied the treasure in her box of clothes, Kassie bounced with excitement and immediately christened them Krystal and Koral. She decided they needed "K names," like the rest of our children. The task of bottle-feeding the kittens and cuddling them was shared by all of the family. However, Krystal decided she belonged to Kassie, and Koral decided she was mine and followed me around like a puppy. To my surprise, the enjoyment the kittens brought strongly decreased the tension in our house, and our curious beagle never touched them.

Kassie had been right. She had needed a kitten to help her be happy again, and so did I. When I was not wise enough to realize that she knew what she needed, God directed the mama cat to a box that already had Kassie's name on it.

(This story was previously printed in *Whispers from Heaven*.)

How many times has a loved one been ill and seemed near death? A situation like this can seem overwhelming to a child. Many would just give in and give up hope. In Deanna's case, however, she did the only thing she knew how to do: She asked the Lord to help her daddy.

One Child's Prayer

BY DEANNA LUKE, FORT WORTH, TEXAS

I was 11 years old in 1958, but I remember the day as clearly as if it were yesterday. It was my last day of summer vacation, and I was enjoying Labor Day with my mother at Aunt Shirley's house. I was watching my uncle pull the steaks off the grill when I heard the phone ring.

"Hello," I heard my aunt say. She hesitated for a moment. "Inez, it's for you."

I watched my mom take the phone. "Hello, this is Inez...yes... I'll be there shortly. Thank you for calling, Danny." Her hands were shaking as she hung up the phone.

"Mom?"

She grasped my hand in hers and we walked into the living room.

Aunt Shirley was the first one to speak. "Is everything all right, Inez?"

"That was Danny. He said there was an accident at the railroad."

"Is Daddy okay?" I could barely get the words out. Everyone waited quietly for her answer.

"He's going to be fine, honey. He's got a broken arm is all."

"What happened?" Aunt Shirley wanted details, and I listened closely.

"Well, evidently he was training a new employee, teaching him how to set a boxcar break. The train came to an abrupt halt unexpectedly, and he was tossed from the train." She went on to explain that as a conductor on the railroad, part of Daddy's job was to train the new men.

We went home immediately, preparing the bedroom for my injured father. While we were putting the dirty sheets into the washer, the phone rang. Mom ran to answer, and I finished loading the laundry. "Hello? I'm on my way," I heard her say. After making a quick phone call to my aunt, we left the bed only partially made, and mom hurried me to the car. We drove back to Aunt Shirley's. "Thank you so much for watching her. I'll be back as soon as I can."

"What did they tell you?" My aunt's look of concern worried me. She squeezed my mom's shoulder and pulled me to her side.

"They said his injuries are worse than they originally thought and he's unconscious."

Mom drove 30 miles to the hospital and called us after she had some answers. Dad had a shattered wrist and a broken hip, among other various injuries.

Days went by and I was desperate to see my dad, but the hospital rule was "No children under 13." Finally, after hearing me cry for days, one of my aunts gave in.

"Come on, Deanna, we're going to the hospital." She cleaned me up and drove me to the hospital. It was the longest 30 minutes of my life.

When we arrived, there was a nun sitting at the receptionist desk, and my aunt explained our situation. The sister shook her head adamantly. *"No!"* I was devastated.

"I want to see whoever's in charge." My aunt was not easily swayed.

The nun, who looked ancient to me and quite capable of enforcing her decisions, seemed to have a change of heart after listening to our story. "I'm going to let you go up just this once," she said, "but you need to show me that you can behave like a grown-up. Do you understand?"

"Yes ma'am…um, Sister." I nodded my head, eager to find my dad's room. My aunt took my hand and whisked me into an elevator before the nun could change her mind.

Arriving at my father's room, I stood frozen at the door for a moment, taking in all the sights and smells around me. The whole place smelled like rubbing alcohol. I walked toward the bed. My dad was in traction. I looked into the corner of the room and saw my mother. She looked so frail sitting there, waiting. She raised her finger to her lips, indicating for me to be quiet. She did not have to remind me. The nun had already made it clear.

"Deanna, I want you to stay here with your dad while I take your mom to another room to take a quick shower. Do you think you can do that?" My aunt was trusting me to do something very grown-up, and I readily agreed. "I want you to sit right here beside him, and don't do anything unless he tells you so." I agreed and they left the room.

I looked at my unmoving father and was terrified by his help-lessness. Tears spilled over onto my face, and I began to pray. "Please, God, please let him wake up. I need my daddy to take care of me. I know You don't need him as much as I do."

While I was praying, I stared at Dad through my tears. His eyes opened! I pressed a button near the bed and kept pressing it until another nun came to the room, looking less than pleased. But I didn't care. "My daddy opened his eyes!" I clasped her hand tightly, pleading for her to stay. "Watch! I know he'll do it again."

"Honey, we all hope he will open his eyes." She didn't believe me, but I knew what I saw. "Just stay here and watch. I know he will.…Look, see! He opened them again!"

The sister's eyes opened wide and she turned all of her attention to my father. She spoke directly to him, and he answered her. I was just a little girl, but God heard my prayers and said, "Okay."

Today, Dad is 88 years old. I will never forget how the Lord honored my desperate prayer that day—the prayer of a simple 11-year-old girl missing the company of her father.

It's sometimes difficult to remain optimistic, especially when missing animals are concerned. As adults we've seen all too often how lost animals end up. Yet in the innocent eyes of a child, nothing is impossible and pessimism is seldom in their vocabulary. Ann learned very quickly how God often uses the tender heart of a child to bring us back to belief in His power.

Coco Comes Home

BY ANN OLIVER, TYLER, TEXAS

One night as I was getting the children ready for bed and ready for our nightly prayers, Judy, my youngest daughter, looked at me and said, "I'm going to pray that Coco comes home."

My heart felt a pang of regret. Coco, our big old tomcat, had been gone a year and the possibility of a return at this date seemed utterly impossible. I did not want my little girl to be disappointed.

I floundered for words, and then I said a very stupid thing, "Oh Judy, God does not have time for dogs and cats!" I regretted the words as soon as I spoke them. She looked up at me and said, "Well I'm going to pray anyway, because you said God always answers our prayers." She bowed her head and prayed. I left the room with a heavy heart, not knowing how I was to handle the disappointment when Coco did not return.

As I was finishing up in the kitchen that night, I heard a commotion outside in the carport. I opened the back door to see what was going on and there was Coco! Wild and disheveled, he was hissing at our other cats.

I was not the only one who heard the commotion; behind me stood Judy and her older sister, Jana, their eyes open wide in surprise.

Judy looked up at me and cried with happiness, "See Mom, God *does* have time for dogs and cats!"

"Yes," I answered her, in utter amazement, "He certainly does."

He also had time to teach a foolish mother a very valuable lesson on prayer.

2
God's Divine Protection

We serve a God who offers us divine protection when we make Him our refuge and our dwelling place. Psalm 91 tells us that no evil shall befall those who are abiding in Him. All that comes to us must pass through His mighty hands first.

What confidence this assurance gives us in times of danger or when our natural reaction is to be afraid of something. Just as Jesus told His disciples, "Fear not," so, too, He offers those same comforting words to us.

If we trust in Him, we have *nothing to fear.*

> *For you have made the LORD, my refuge,*
> *Even the Most High, your dwelling place.*
> *No evil will befall you,*
> *Nor will any plague come near your tent.*
> *For He will give His angels charge concerning you,*
> *To guard you in all your ways* (Psalm 91:9-11 NASB).

Prayer can be the source of comfort in hours of great fear. It can bring peace to a heart that is pounding with fright. Rich discovered that peace and, as a result of one awful, life-threatening event, made a life-changing decision.

A Night of Peril

BY SUSAN M. FOSTER, LAGUNA NIGUEL, CALIFORNIA
(AS TOLD BY RICHARD ANDERSON)

"Wallets, car keys, jewelry, valuables...*now!*"

Two masked robbers brandished guns at the seven of us huddled in the small storage room at the rear of the recording studio.

"Don't kill us," I pleaded in desperation. "We have families and..."

"Do you think we care about your personal lives?" the second thug snarled. "A recording studio is soundproof. No one will hear the gunshots."

My heart lurched. *Dear God, will we live to see another day?* I prayed.

Cursing, the two men bound our feet and wrists with layers of duct tape, secured our wrists with electrical cords, and taped our mouths shut.

Just a few hours earlier, the six members of our band, Southland, met our engineer at a recording studio in Brea, California, to record a CD. We ordered pizza for dinner and were waiting for it to arrive. When one of the guys stepped outside to check on our pizza delivery, the armed robbers hurled him back into the room. In shock, I dropped my 800-dollar Takamine guitar.

The thugs ordered us to line up against the wall.

One of our guys, Vance, was a police officer, and I thought he might have some kind of remote-control device to activate, calling for backup. Searching Vance's face for some sign of reassurance, I was dismayed to see his petrified look. "Oh, Lord! He's as powerless as the rest of us," I murmured, suddenly feeling weak and lightheaded.

The thugs forcibly herded us from the recording studio into the small rear storage room. An emergency-exit door momentarily held a dawning ray of hope. Freedom and the outside world beckoned just beyond. Two fellow band members slammed their weight against the door in a vain attempt at making a break for freedom. It was bolted illegally from the outside. There was no way of escape, and any hope we had was slipping away.

Without warning, I was snapped back into the present by a cruel blow to my face. I realized it was my turn to be tied up. Evidently upset that he had run out of duct tape, the thug decided to take his frustration out on me. My jaw throbbed from the blow, and the electrical cord dug into my flesh as he tied my hands behind my back. The duct tape already across my mouth made it difficult to breathe, and I was feeling claustrophobic. *As bad as this is, I know it's going to get worse.*

We were paired up, tied together face-to-face, and ordered to lie down execution-style. My partner, Ron, and I toppled over sideways. I found myself facedown on the carpet, unable to see anything. Hurling expletives, our captors exited the storage room. For a time, our group was left alone. But as the robbers gathered up our sound equipment, I heard them check in on us every few minutes.

My face pressed into the coarse carpet, I prepared myself to die. I imagined my family having to live with painful memories surrounding my demise. While reflecting on my lost opportunity to experience the growing up of my two preteen sons, I felt a profound sense of sadness. *Never again will Andy, Evan, and I ride bikes together. No more cheering for my boys at baseball games. Never again will we play catch in the park. No proud dad to celebrate their high school graduations. Never again to...*

My thoughts revolved around speculation as to where the bullet would enter my body and how it would feel to die. *I wonder if they'll shoot me in the back or in the head. Will I go fast, or will it be lingering and painful?*

During the intervals when the robbers were preoccupied in the sound room, I fervently petitioned the Lord for a miracle. To strengthen and encourage myself, I also recited in my head a favorite Scripture verse: "Never will I leave you; never will I forsake you" (Hebrews 13:5).

Gradually, we assisted each other in pulling the duct tape down below our mouths and were able to communicate in hushed tones.

"Hey, Rich," Ron whispered to me, "did you feel that strange fanning sensation a few minutes back?"

"Yeah, I did. But it stopped when the guys left the room."

"I'm not crazy. I think there are angels here with us," Ron said.

"I think so, too. It's like I can feel the presence of God—an incredible peace, you know?"

Never will I leave you; never will I forsake you. God's promise resounded through my mind.

"Me, too!" Ron replied. "I'm not scared in the least."

Something had changed—an incredible peace and a realization that we would get out of this alive seemed to course through all of us. As the robbers began checking on our group less frequently, we agreed to take action. Quietly, Vance urged us, "Listen, you guys. We can't just lie here helpless on the floor waiting to die. We've got to fight back!"

"You're right," I responded. "Let's see if we can help each other up and somehow untie ourselves." Although seemingly impossible, we were able to snap each other's duct tape and electrical cords apart in mere seconds. Without question, divine intervention was at work.

"All right, guys, this is our chance!" Vance gave us direction. "A couple of you charge the rear door. The rest of us will grab chairs for self-defense. Okay, at the count of three, go!"

Slamming their bodies against the bolted door, just as they had done earlier, two fellow band members miraculously broke it down. Free at last, we scattered and summoned the police. Within minutes, what seemed like the entire police force was on the scene. It seemed the robbers had escaped out the front door as soon as they heard the back door crashing down.

Although our whole ordeal had only lasted 45 minutes, our interviews with the police at the crime scene continued well into the night. We lost thousands of dollars of equipment, as well as personal effects that were never recovered. After months of investigation, the case remains unsolved. I have no regrets about the loss of my possessions. I am grateful to be alive.

This 1997 robbery was, without question, a life-changing event for me. While lying on the floor, preparing to die, I realized how fragile life really is and how it literally could be over in seconds. I also know God is the One who decides when it's time for us to go. I also promised Him that if I made it out alive, my life, beginning the very next day, would be different. I resolved to develop a committed relationship with the Lord. I wanted to be used as an instrument to touch people's lives through active ministry. I was ready to listen to what God wanted from me, not what I wanted from Him.

Looking back on my life following this experience, I am acutely aware of the hand of God. In fact, four years after this horrendous ordeal, I entered the ministry full-time to pastor Capistrano Community Church in San Juan Capistrano, California. I took my promise to the Lord seriously, and I have been blessed for it. I believe in the power of prayer.

And I believe, without a doubt, that God both protected and delivered us that night.

Colonel Hanson knew danger could be found in almost every corner of Kuwait. With war just about to begin, he knew that praying for God to keep them safe in the "palm of His hand" was not a choice, but a necessity.

Cliff-hanger

BY CLEMENT HANSON, RETIRED COLONEL,
UNITED STATES ARMY, DENVER, COLORADO

Lieutenant Arno Kivi and I had just arrived back at our compound from battalion headquarters on a warm January evening. Six weeks in the Saudi Arabian desert, as part of the United States Third Armored Division's medical company gave us plenty of reasons to try and get some rest.

That evening I lay down on my cot and opened my worn Bible to a favorite verse of mine, Isaiah 41:10 (NIV): "So do not fear, for I am with you; do not be dismayed, for I am your God. I will strengthen you and help you; I will uphold you with my righteous right hand."

The Army Central Command operations plan called for a five-week, massive air campaign against the Iraqi Army occupying Kuwait. Rumors were flying that the air war would begin any day.

I took a deep breath. "Please, God, keep us in Your right hand. Watch over us and protect us." After I finished praying, I settled in for a little sleep.

"Doctor Hanson?" The tent canvas shook as a communications specialist crawled inside. "There's a call for you on the field phone from the major over at battalion headquarters. He says it's important."

I pulled on my boots, picked up my Colt .45 and gas mask, and hurried to the medical company headquarters tent.

"Doctor Hanson here."

"You need to get over here right away to inspect a case of meals-ready-to-eat. Some soldiers from the Bravo Company said they got sick from eating them, and I have a case of MRE's in my office, waiting for inspection."

I drew a deep breath. "We'll be there tonight, Major."

I headed to the tent where Lieutenant Kivi lay sound asleep. He woke with a start when I put my hand on his shoulder. "Arno, we need to inspect some MRE's tonight at battalion headquarters. I just got off the phone with the major."

Arno groaned. He switched on his flashlight and squinted to see his watch. "Well, we might as well get over there right away, before it gets any later."

"How long will it take to get there, do the inspection, and get back here?" Arno was more familiar with the distances than I was.

He thought for a moment. "Shouldn't be more than an hour or two. There's enough light from the stars and moon for us to follow the Green Supply Route barrel markers." He sat up and reached for his boots. "I'll get Sergeant Vickie Vernardo to come with me. She's done a lot of field ration inspections." He began to get dressed.

"I think I'll come along with you and the Sergeant. I hear the major is a terror with junior officers and enlisted people. If I come along, we should get back quicker."

The three of us Humveed out the front gate at 9:15 P.M. The desert sky was partly cloudy, with no wind or rain. Lieutenant Kivi drove, Sergeant Vernardo sat in the back, and I navigated with my wrist compass while sitting in the right front seat. We bounced over the rocky desert terrain with only dim blackout lights providing illumination over the barren ground ahead of us. Mandatory light discipline required us to drive with no more than blackout lights at night to avoid detection by Iraqi forces.

The major was waiting for us in the battalion operations center. "About time!" His voice was threatening. "I thought you got lost."

"We got here as quick as we could, sir. Now if I could get one of those MRE's to take back with us to our compound tonight, I'll inspect it tomorrow during the daylight hours. I also need to get the lot numbers and call the unit when we get back to see if they have any more of the same meals."

"Well, I guess that will have to do, Doctor." I was glad I made the trip for the sake of my comrades.

We left battalion headquarters at about 10:00 P.M. with the MRE's. As we drove northwest into the darkening desert, Arno hummed a tune. As the minutes stretched to a half hour, gathering clouds hid the moon and stars. The wind began to pick up, and visibility became limited.

After a while, I could see well enough to find the green barrels marking our route back. I switched on my red-lens flashlight and pointed it to my field compass. "Turn a little more to your north, Arno."

He turned the steering wheel about 30 degrees counterclockwise. The three of us strained our eyes to find a barrel or anything that would stand out from the empty terrain. Nothing. We were lost.

Kivi slowed the Humvee to about five miles per hour. The landscape became rougher and the clouds gathered lower. We couldn't see anything except the blackness of the night. As we drove along, my eyelids grew heavy, and my chin slumped to my chest.

Arno slammed on the brakes!

I bolted upright in my seat. "What's wrong?"

"Sir, you yelled at me to stop the Humvee."

I rubbed my eyes. "No I didn't."

"Sir, I distinctly heard you yell at me to stop."

Sergeant Vernardo woke up. "What's going on?"

We strained our tired eyes to look ahead through the front windshield. Beyond the Humvee's front bumper, the ground disappeared.

"Arno, take a deep breath, shift into reverse, and ease your foot off the brake."

He shifted into reverse and backed us up about ten feet, where the three of us climbed out of our vehicle. We switched on our red-lens field flashlights and shined them forward, and then down into the darkness. We were standing on the edge of a cliff on a ridge of sand dunes. We all peered down in disbelief. The ground plummeted at least a hundred feet into black-velvet darkness. Another few feet forward and we would have disappeared over the edge. There were no seatbelts in the Humvee, so we would have all been ejected through the front windshield.

After our shock, we all climbed quietly back into the vehicle. I swallowed hard. "Arno, I wonder who yelled at you to hit the brakes. It wasn't Sergeant Vernardo or me. We were both sleeping."

Arno pulled a U-turn and headed west and south. After about 15 minutes, we made out the shape of a lone barrel, and then another in the distance. Finally we had found the supply route!

By midnight we entered the front gate of our perimeter. We pulled up to our tent and climbed out of our Humvee. Exhausted, we were relieved to be back to our compound.

The next morning, we found out that there was a ridge of sand dunes with a cliff overhanging a deep ravine in the Third Armored Division area. We were the first soldiers in the division to find it, and in complete darkness.

I remembered hearing over Armed Forces Radio several months prior that the first American fatality of Desert Storm had occurred when a U.S. Marine captain drove a Humvee over the cliff of a sand dune.

Unknowingly we had made the same mistake as the Marine captain; however, unlike the captain, we survived our encounter with the drop-off.

It was then that the clear, unmistakable message came to me: God's hand was at the wheel of our Humvee that night. I had prayed that He would protect us and keep us in His right hand. He did, and He spared our lives in a miraculous way.

When our child's life is in danger, there is little we would not do in order to save him or her. Topmost on our list is to ask God for His help. In the case of little Nancy, her parents knew that prayer was their only hope.

Angels Watching over Little Nancy

BY GLORIA CASSITY STARGEL, GAINESVILLE, GEORGIA
(AS TOLD BY SUE JONES)

Darkness was closing in as I maneuvered my old Dodge Charger down the treacherous road around Blood Mountain. I had just completed my shift at Union County Medical Center in Blairsville and started the hour-and-a-half drive home. My major concern was getting home safely that November Friday afternoon. Then my pager sounded. Beep! "You're to call this number in Dahlonega," the voice on the other end said.

"Dahlonega?" I wondered aloud. Fear took hold. My husband, Don, had taken the children hiking toward Dahlonega, but they would have been home hours ago.

I dialed the number and heard, "Lumpkin County Sheriff's Office." Suddenly I felt sick to my stomach.

"This is Sue Jones," I said, panic building. "What's wrong?"

"You need to get down here right away."

I started to cry. "Tell me what's wrong."

"Ma'am, you've got to come down here. One of your children is missing."

Dear God, help me.

A friend drove me to Dahlonega. During the hour-long drive, unanswered questions pounded inside my head. *Which child? What happened? A kidnapping? What?*

I shot out of the car when we arrived and ran smack into a bevy of media people with cameras and microphones in hand. The sheriff rushed out and escorted me into his office.

I was becoming hysterical. "Where are my babies? I want to see my babies!"

"Matthew and Rachel are in a back office," he replied, "playing with a computer and eating cookies. But your youngest, the two-year-old, is missing."

"Nancy? Nancy is missing? What are you saying? Someone took my baby?" I felt totally out of control.

"Your husband said she wandered off while they were hiking. She's lost in the forest."

"Lost? Nancy is lost in the forest? My baby is alone in those mountains? It's cold out there. And dark. And raining. And there are wild animals! We've got to find her! Take me there!" I demanded.

"We have crews searching, Mrs. Jones. It would be best if you stayed here."

"Where is my husband? Where is Don? Is he out there searching? I want to see Don!" I needed my husband desperately. I needed his steadying strength.

"Mr. Jones is here, but you can't see him right now. We're questioning him, trying to find out what happened."

By nine o'clock, the officers surrendered to my frenzied pleas and drove me out through the rugged terrain to the Chattahoochee National Forest. We passed a roadblock and came to a stop. An old logging trail snaked precariously around the side of a mountain.

"This is where Mr. Jones parked his car this morning," the officer told me. "He said the children stopped to play in a clearing about a mile and a half down this trail. He took his eyes off them for a minute. That's when little Nancy disappeared."

"I'm going in there," I said, lunging out of the car and heading toward the steep path. "She'll know my voice and answer me."

"We can't let you do that." A firm hand grabbed my shoulder. "You need be here when we bring her out."

I resisted, but the officer stood firm. I called out across the black forest, "Nancy! Nancy! Mommy's here, baby. Come to Mommy." My voice was devoured by the vast darkness.

Across the valley, I saw a long line of lights moving slowly through the trees. *The searchers!* "Dear God, please help them find my baby."

Beautiful little Nancy had just turned two years old—Nancy, with her precious pixie smile, those big brown eyes, her light-brown hair, and a bright ribbon tied on top of her sweet head. "Please, God, send Your angels to look after Nancy," I prayed.

In the patrol car, I could hear communication between the staging area and the searchers in the woods. Every radio crackle made me hold my breath. At one point, an army helicopter was brought in, giving me hope. Its heat sensors located two coon hunters and a deer, but no little girl.

Search dogs arrived. They were led down the logging trail in teams of two, not making a sound. "The dogs will find her if anything can," someone said. But they didn't.

I shivered in the night air. The temperature dropped to 40 degrees. *Please, God, if they don't find her right away, put her into a deep sleep so she won't feel anything, so she won't feel fear, or cold, or pain.*

And especially, dear Lord, so she won't think her mommy and daddy aban-doned her. It just about killed me to think she might feel we did not love her.

About midnight, two friends were allowed into the forest with me. They put their arms around me and prayed. It was three o'clock in the morning before Don was brought out to the site. He brought shocking news with him. "Honey, they think I did something to her."

"What?" I was incredulous.

"They've been interrogating me all this time. They kept asking why I had my rifle with me. I tried to explain I never go into the forest without my rifle. I use it for protection. There are bears in the woods, and coyote. In fact, if I hadn't had my rifle, I couldn't have signaled for help."

Don was a loving, devoted father to our children. We held each other and cried.

Just before dawn, the sheriff drove us home to get Nancy's bed linens so the dogs could pick up her scent. I couldn't watch as the men donned rubber gloves, removed her sheets and pillowcase, and placed them in a plastic bag. Hours ticked by, and a steady rain cast a dreary pall over the day. I began to experience an indescribable mental agony. Eventually, my anguished prayers began to include, "Lord, I don't need to know the why of this. And whether I like the result or not, help me to accept it. Lord, I just pray that You will give Don and me peace. But most of all, I pray you will give Nancy peace in her little heart."

Among God's angels in heaven, there must have been a great flutter of wings when prayers for Nancy came in. The Master's plan began to unfold.

9:00 A.M. Kip Clayton, a guard with the Lee Arrendale Correctional Institute, gets a call. His volunteer unit, Habersham County High Angel Rescue Team, is needed to search for a two-year-old girl in the Chattahoochee National Forest. "Oh, dear God. That's the age of my own little girl." He gathers his gear and heads out.

10:00 A.M. Al Stowers, a physician with an Atlanta hospital, is hiking in the Amicalola Falls area, 25 miles away. "Looking for some of life's answers," he says later. When he switches on his pocket-size radio, he hears, "Little Nancy Jones is still lost in the forest." Dr. Stowers just "happens" to specialize in trauma and pediatric medicine. Besides that, he has just returned from Alaska where he received special training in hypothermia. He knows Nancy's time is quickly running out. "I've got to help find her." He hurries to his vehicle.

1:50 P.M. Back at the search area, more than 200 professionals and volunteers are combing the forest. They are told to make one more sweep. Hope is running out fast, and they will be forced to abandon the effort.

Making that final sweep, Kip Clayton leads his search team to the outer limit of their assigned area. Reluctantly, he turns to begin his sweep back. But wait…"Something" tells him to go an additional 250 yards. He does. "Then I turn and take two steps," he says. "She is lying five feet in front of me." Shocked, he yells to his teammates, "I see her!"

Kip fears she is dead. She is lying so still, facedown in wet leaves and mud, "Just as close up against a log as she could get." Then a tiny whimper, almost like a sigh, comes from the little soaked body. "She's alive!" he shouts into the radio. "She's alive!" Awed, Kip knew in his heart, *God led me right to her.*

1:50 P.M. Just seconds earlier, Dr. Stowers arrives at the staging area. He is turned away as "not needed." He scribbles his car phone number down anyway and leaves it behind. He has the motor running and his car in gear when someone runs toward him. "Don't leave. We've found her! She's alive!" He reaches the ambulance in time to see it is a "load and go" situation. "I'm right behind you," he calls out to the driver. They both speed off toward the local hospital.

In the patrol car, Don and I hear Kip's shouts over the radio. "She's alive! She's alive!" Relief and gratitude fill my being. "Oh, Don. She's alive."

"They're rushing her to the hospital by ambulance," an excited officer tells us. "Meet them at St. Joseph!"

We beat them there. As they hurry into the emergency room, I call out to the little form inside the huge cocoon of blankets, "Nancy, baby. Mommy and Daddy are here. We love you!"

Nancy is pronounced critical. She is unconscious, swollen, and blue. Her temperature registers 74 degrees. Her heart rate is just 70 beats per minute. "I doubt if she could have survived out there another two hours," Dr. Stowers tells us. We pray.

Dr. Stowers and the local medical team work feverishly to stabilize Nancy enough for transport to Egleston Children's Hospital in Atlanta for more intensive care. Dr. Stowers asks the director of nurses, "Can you get me a pediatric nurse to travel with us?" Gale Blankenship, a highly skilled nurse who works p.r.n. (as needed) locally and regular weekend duty at Scottish-Rite Children's Hospital in Atlanta, just "happens" not to have left for work yet. When Gale calls the Atlanta hospital and explains the emergency, a co-worker "is led" to work an extra shift so Gale can help Nancy.

An hour later, in the ambulance transporting Nancy to Egleston, space is tight. They tuck us in around her. Sherrie, the respiratory specialist, sits at Nancy's head, operating the breathing bag. An EMT, sitting at her left side, checks all the equipment. The pediatric nurse, Gale, is to her right, keeping the IV tubes functioning. Dr. Stowers, at her feet, watches the heart monitor. They position me so I can talk to her and pat her little head, which is barely visible above the heated-air blanket.

Nancy's temperature does not yet register on the thermometer. She continues to be unresponsive. But wait! Do I detect a movement in her fingers? I gently lay my index finger in her hand and weakly, very weakly, her little fingers close around it. Midway to Atlanta, Nancy's eyes flutter. "Mama."

We all gasp. I continue to gently stroke her forehead, whispering, "Nancy, baby. Mommy's here."

"Mama, song," she says, in a faintly audible voice.

I know what she wants. I start singing softly, "Jesus loves me this I know, for the Bible tells me so...." Sherrie sings, too. Unbelievably, little Nancy, through swollen and chapped lips, tries to join in. I look around at the circle of amazed expressions. Dr. Stowers makes no effort to hide the huge tears spilling down his face. Nor do we.

Dear Jesus, who loves Nancy, *thank You, thank You, and thank You!*

On arrival at Egleston, Nancy's condition was still listed as critical. She was not yet fully conscious and slept through most of Sunday. She woke up on Monday, her normal self! Don laughingly describes it: "She perked right up and trashed the room." Later that day, she *walked* to the car. Our little family came home together.

I can never say thank you enough to all those who took time from their busy lives to rescue little Nancy. They have my undying gratitude and my prayers. May they be blessed beyond measure.

In the future, if ever I wonder whether or not God hears and answers prayers, I will remember this experience. For only God and His ministering angels could have orchestrated such a miraculous set of circumstances. Yes, He hears...and answers.

3
All Creatures Great and Small

Aren't you glad God created animals? Anyone who can look at a giraffe and not smile at God's sense of humor on the fifth day of Creation needs an immediate funny-bone transplant.

In the Bible, God used animals occasionally to fulfill His purposes. Just ask Jonah. Or consider the story of Balaam's donkey in Numbers 22. We also know that the Lord Jesus chose a colt on which to ride triumphantly into Jerusalem on Palm Sunday.

Today God still uses animals, as the following stories illustrate, or as almost anyone who has ever had a beloved pet can testify.

> *Then God said, "Let the earth bring forth living creatures after their kind: cattle and creeping things and beasts of the earth after their kind"; and it was so. God made the beasts of the earth after their kind, and the cattle after their kind, and everything that creeps on the ground after its kind; and God saw that it was good* (Genesis 1:24-25 NASB).

God often sends the most unexpected teachers into our lives. During a season of Wendy's life when answers to her most heart-wrenching questions were hard to find, she would come to learn a powerful truth. As Benjy grew in obedience to his master, so too did Wendy grow in obedience to her God as trust replaced turmoil.

Do You Trust Me?

BY WENDY DELLINGER, LAKEWOOD, COLORADO

Looking both ways, my husband and I dashed across the rain-soaked street from the animal shelter to our car. I wrapped our new ten-week-old border collie puppy in a protective hug against the raw Colorado spring weather, but I could feel him quiver. As we settled into the car, he pressed deeply into my lap. "It's okay," I soothed. "You're going home now."

I stroked him for reassurance, feeling the matted and dirty fur. So much for the bath the kennel had promised. "Whew," my husband muttered, cracking a window for fresh air. "Kinda overpowering." Considering this little guy's short history, I could forgive him. He had been found only days before in a dumpster with his eight siblings and wild, snarling mother, and had been rescued with some drama. Glancing down into his intelligent little face, I was glad we were part of his redemption.

Driving home, the dripping chill of the day sent a shiver through me. The puppy's warmth felt good, and I drew him closer. *Strange how things work out,* I thought with a heavy sigh, *after all our dreams of getting a house, having a family, of watching kids and a dog happily romping together in a grassy yard.*

Lord, I'm having such a hard time with this, I prayed. *You know I'm thankful for the house. It was worth the long wait. But God, why are my arms only filled with a dog and not my children? How could You have permitted such losses when I trusted You, believing Your promises to me? Miscarriage...stillbirth. Ugly words that I can't believe You allowed to happen to me. Why aren't there any answers? How do I keep on trusting? I'm trying, Lord, but my heart feels dead. How do I go on? Or maybe the better question is, How do I go on with You?*

The puppy stirred in my lap and laid his head on my arm, pulling me back from the well-worn path of grief and confusion that I walked in my mind, day after day. I smiled down at him, in spite of my oppressive thoughts. *This little fellow needs us,* I thought, *and we need him. Yes, I'm glad we found him.*

Now I have always considered myself a cat person, so the days that followed were a new adventure for me. He learned to answer quickly to his new name, Benjy, and soon forgot his dark beginnings. There were very few steps I could take in any direction that he was not invisibly tethered to me. I lived on the floor, cuddling him in my lap or playing tug-of-war with an old sock, laughing sometimes to tears at his hilarious antics. And with my husband gone all day at work, the task of dog training fell to me.

Truth to tell, I knew almost nothing about training a dog. But I figured that the methods my parents had used with me would more or less work with him. Fortunately (for me!), Benjy was smart, and after only one or two sessions on a particular command, he had it.

However, we had difficulty with "Stay." He always wanted to come. *Okay,* I thought one morning. *We're just going to work at this until we get it.* After an initial demonstration, I placed him at one end of the room, moved to the other end, and commanded, "Stay!" He dutifully trotted to me in happy excitement, eyes shining. "No, no," I said, shaking a finger in his face. I carried him back and set him down firmly with another "Benjy, stay!" He dropped low, this time creeping slowly back to me, ears down.

Trying not to laugh, I picked him up, deposited him for the third time, and said in a stern and very disapproving voice, "No, no! Bad dog! Stay!" He dropped, head between his paws, and this time he stayed.

"Good dog!" I cried jubilantly. "You did it!" I patted my leg for his return.

But this time, he didn't move. He lay there, head down on his paws, large brown eyes staring at me, ears hanging very low. "Come, Benjy," I urged brightly, patting my leg again. He still didn't move. Puzzled, I called him again. He gave not a flicker of response—just that reproachful, unblinking stare. Now I could not persuade him to come. We stared at each other in a silent impasse as I deliberated. *What is going on in that puppy mind?* I thought. *Maybe he's afraid to try again, confused at my contradictions of "Stay" and "Come." Or could it be my sternness? Maybe he thinks I'm angry with him, that I don't love him anymore.*

I ran and scooped him up with a fierce hug to reassure him. "Silly boy," I said, kissing his head. "I'm not mad at you. I love you! I know what I'm doing. You've just got to trust me."

I stopped abruptly. In a flash of revelation, I heard God's voice echoing my own words back to me.

"You've just got to trust Me."

The training scene before me was suddenly, and most graphically, a training session between God and me. Were we so very different, Benjy and I? He didn't know that I could be trusted, even if he didn't wholly understand what I wanted of him. But isn't that just what I had done with God? All that I had ever learned of Him in the Bible told me He could be trusted, even in the mysteries of suffering. Yet my bruised faith, wounded and afraid, was holding Him at a distance.

Maybe the answer to my "Why?" was not the real issue. Maybe it was my faith. I needed to make a choice to trust again because I belonged to an utterly trustworthy Master. All things work together for good…beauty for ashes…joy comes in the morning…a future and a hope. Those promises He had once spoken to my heart were still His words. In spite of the seeming contradictions of my life, He was asking me to believe because His heart was for my good, just as mine was for Benjy. Maybe it was time to take His hand again, to walk this thing out together.

With tears of thankfulness, I gave Benjy another hug. He jumped and licked my face with humbling eagerness in reply. "Okay," I said, "let's try this again." I took him to the end of the room, commanded him to stay, and walked back to my place. This time he stayed perfectly until I said, "Come!" With happy understanding, he raced back to me. "Good boy!" I cried. "You got it!" We tumbled together on the floor, and I laughed at the joy of reconciliation and renewed trust, his and mine.

In the months that followed, Benjy grew to be a handsome dog and much-loved member of our family. I, too, grew, not in stature but in grace. God's peace settled down in my heart to stay, and though it did not happen overnight, I knew my faith had weathered the storm and, like the seasoned tree, was stronger for it. Then one spring, when new life was awakening in the earth around us, I gave birth to a beautiful daughter. As sure as the sunrise, God had brought about His good and loving purposes for me, just as He had promised.

Often on a summer's night, we are in the backyard throwing Frisbees, playing keep-away with Benjy. My husband and I laugh as we watch our daughter and Benjy race and chase together, buddies to the core. *Surely, joy does come in the morning*, I smile to myself, *even though God might use a puppy-training session to do it.*

Patience is in short supply in our ever-changing, fast-paced world. It is difficult enough to exhibit patience in raising children, and sometimes even more difficult when a pet enters the picture. Joan prayed for patience—patience to handle an animal she had never wanted in the first place.

Life Is Precious Where There Is Love

BY JOAN CLAYTON, PORTALES, NEW MEXICO

"Not another dog!"

"But he's such a nice dog," my husband, Emmitt, said, patting the creature defensively.

"This dog is not going to be a house dog," and I meant it. Chalk one up for the only case I won concerning this new family member.

Emmitt named him "Bear." *He looks like one and acts like one,* I thought. I tried not to like this cuddly little puppy. His little brown mustache, attached to a black-and-brown spotted body with a short tail that never stopped wagging, made it hard for me to dislike him.

Winter came and, although it brought mild temperatures, Emmitt thought Bear might be cold, so periodically he let Bear in to get warm. Bear's hyperactive nature took over big time. His running here and there and knocking things around did not make me too happy.

To keep the peace, Emmitt picked Bear up one day and rocked him in the rocking chair. This became a daily ritual. Did you ever hear of a grown man rocking a dog? Bear soon learned a trick in the middle of the night that woke up the neighborhood.

"Woo-ooo-ooo-ooo!" Like a baby, he wanted to be rocked.

I went to the vet, and he gave me a dog tranquilizer to put in Bear's meat, but the next morning poor Bear seemed to be hung over from the tranquilizer, so I didn't do that anymore.

The howling was bad enough, but as Bear grew, things in our backyard began to disintegrate. First, my beautiful flowering plum tree came down. He chewed the trunk right in two. Then he dug ugly holes everywhere and scattered firewood from the woodpile all over the yard.

"Look at that yard," I complained.

"But he's such a good dog." Emmitt loved that dog.

That's when my prayers for this situation began in earnest. "Lord, give me patience for this dog," I prayed. "Help me to see my husband's love for Your creatures."

I accidentally found out that Bear had chewed up all the wiring on Emmitt's horse trailer. He hadn't told me. It would have added more fuel to the fire.

One day I really exploded when I discovered that Bear had chewed up all the satellite wiring to our television set. Emmitt tried to keep ahead of Bear's destructive habits.

My growing impatience reminded me of my prayer for patience. Guarding my tongue became a challenge, and I worked hard at keeping the peace. After all, I had prayed for patience.

Leaving for church one day, we noticed Bear had the volleyball in his mouth.

"What a fun dog you are," Emmitt said, patting his head. "Go ahead and play."

We returned from church to find Bear still standing at the back door with his teeth stuck tight in the volleyball. Emmitt picked up the ball, and Bear came with it. He had to literally pry Bear's mouth out of the ball. I couldn't help but laugh, and I had to admit I had begun to love that dog.

In spite of my aggravation, Bear's sweet disposition had won me over. I watched Bear and Emmitt grow even closer as Bear stayed right by his side, and that touched me. This loving, caring man's love for one of God's creatures and my prayer for patience had at last softened my heart.

Bear began to have severe ear infections. After months of surgery and medications, Bear died. We both cried, but Emmitt's pain remained for several weeks. How we missed Bear.

I prayed, "Lord, thank You for the gift of animals. And You know Emmitt has a tender spot for them, so could You send another dog?" I could hardly believe I was praying that prayer.

"I'm going to town," Emmitt said one day. As he kissed me goodbye, he remarked, "This is a special day." I thought, "*He finally remembered this is Valentine's Day,* and I dreamed of him bringing home a beautiful valentine.

Later that afternoon, Emmitt walked into the house grinning.

"Where have you been?" I noticed a twinkle in his eye.

"Come see. I have a Valentine for you," he said, leading me to the backyard.

My "Valentine" was brown and black and looked like Bear's brother. I fell in love with those big, beautiful black eyes, and we named him "Valentine."

Valentine rushed to me with more love than I deserved.

God had answered my prayers in ways I had not anticipated. I believe God used Bear to teach me humility, compassion, love for His creatures, and most of all…patience.

I am thankful for the lesson Bear and Emmitt taught me, but more than that, the lesson God taught me: Life is precious where there is love.

Many prayers have been sent to heaven requesting the assistance of angels. God has answered these prayers time and time again. Susan learned that angels could come in many forms, and not just the two-legged variety.

Angel with an Attitude

BY SUSAN FARR FAHNCKE, KAYSVILLE, UTAH

Dear Father in Heaven,

Angel doesn't have much time left. She is so lonely. Her husband never comes to see her, and I would do anything to help make her happier. Please send my sister someone or something to ease her heart. Please help us to give her back her smile.

In Jesus' name I pray. Amen.

At only 28, my baby sister, Angel, was dying from a brain tumor. Abandoned by her husband, her pain was the deepest imaginable. If there was anything, anything at all that would put a smile on her sad and hopeless face, we would do it. So when she asked for a kitten, we leapt at the possibility that this could help ease her loneliness. Cancer is a lonely disease, no matter how many people love and care for you, and sometimes an animal can be a great comfort. So our mother set off in search of Angel's kitten—and she found one.

When the old, grouchy, and loud cat first arrived, my sister hated him. This was clearly not the cute, new kitten she had wanted. It was not a fluffy, adorable baby. It was huge and "argued" with everything in dour tones as ornery as Angel's. Given Angel's sometimes sour moods, I figured them to be kindred spirits. It took Angel a little longer to make the connection. It took "Oreo" a while also. This black-and-white "buddy" for Angel wanted nothing to do with her, nor she with him.

Until the day Angel fell.

Her morning caregiver didn't show up, and Angel was so happy to have some "alone time" that she did not call me or anyone else to let us know. Because her brain tumor had paralyzed her entire right side, she often fell, so she could never be left alone.

I pulled up in the late morning and noticed all the blinds were still shut and immediately knew something was wrong. Running to the door, heart racing, I unlocked it. The first thing I saw was the pool of blood by the door. Rushing to Angel's room, I found her unconscious, the right side of her face and head cut and swollen. Oreo was standing right on top of her, "yelling" at me as if to say "Where have you been?" His back was arched, his face intently watching her as I stumbled through her door. He was rigid and protective, and if a cat can have a worried expression, this one did.

Angel was never the same after that fall, and her time on earth drew to an end only a few months later. But after her fall, her guardian feline never left her side.

Whenever I was able to get her into the living room for some sunshine and a new view, Oreo followed us. The second I got her seated or lying down, he climbed gracefully to his place of guardianship: wrapped around her neck. With disdain, he would glare at anyone who tried to move him, including Angel, so she just got used to having an animal wrapped around her neck at all times.

I don't think she envisioned a "buddy" as committed as this one, but I had to admit, the cat had tenacity. I watched as she smiled at this cranky protector, and I knew she had come to love him just as he had come to love her. Although Oreo was not exactly what I had envisioned when I asked God for an answer to her loneliness, he was God's answer.

As time went by and Angel became too weak to leave her bed, Oreo remained draped across her chest and neck, leaving only for eating and brief visits outside. He slept continually in the same place. We often had to shove him off Angel's face so she could breathe. Guided by God's hand, those two became bonded in what can only be called a miracle.

During Angel's last 24 hours on earth, Oreo did not leave his "spot" on my sister once. He never ate, never went outside, and never moved from his place. Somehow he knew her time was near, and he was determined to be her protector until God took his place and brought her home. Angel died surrounded by people who loved her, my mother's home overflowing with love and people saying good-bye. And Oreo was with her to the last breath.

I miss my sister painfully, but know she is in God's care and I will see her again. I am not the only one that misses her. When I visit our mother, Oreo always seems to be restless, lost without Angel. They had indeed ended up being true kindred spirits. He might have seemed to be disappointing at first, but in the end he was a true-blue, fierce, and loyal protector—a black-and-white cranky "angel with an attitude," and our unexpected answer to prayer.

Lessons on the power of prayer can be seen every day. We can even learn a lesson from the small creatures who fly through our skies and sometimes visit our own front porch.

Sunday School Lesson on the Front Porch

BY CHERYL SCOTT NORWOOD, CANTON, GEORGIA

Sunday afternoon was gloriously beautiful. We had the front door of our little cottage open, with just the half-glass, half-screen door between the outdoors and us. Just off our little front stoop we have several bird feeders, and at one point over 30 little goldfinches were devouring thistle seed.

Suddenly we heard a loud thud! It was so startling that my husband ran in from the back study. "What was that?" he asked. I had a sinking feeling that one of the little goldfinches had flown into the glass part of the door, even though I had positioned sun-catchers on the glass to prevent accidental collisions.

I was right.

"It's a little female finch, honey, and she's hurt," I said to Mike. She was still breathing, and I could see her little wings moving slightly. She was lying in the center of our stoop, where she would be easy prey for neighborhood cats.

Now I love cats and am owned by one myself, but I keep our cat indoors or on a leash as our law states, but some of my neighbors are not as courteous. "Mike, we can't just leave her there. She'll get eaten." "Maybe we should just put her out of her misery, Cheryl," he said to me. "She hit pretty hard—harder than I have ever heard one hit a window. She's not going to make it."

"Well, we should let God decide on whether she lives or dies, not us," I protested. Then we both prayed for our feathery visitor.

"We'll give her a half hour, but if she is still not able to move, we are going to have to be merciful, sweetheart," Mike said, "and I will take care of it. I know you can't do it." I scooped her up gently and put her in a pile of leaves to the side of the stoop. I could observe her from a window, but she would be out of sight from the rest of the yard. There she could be watched and protected from the neighborhood feline ruffians.

I sat there in the window, watching and waiting. Soon a bright-yellow male goldfinch came within a couple inches of our patient. He began to chirp a few notes every minute or two, as if to say, "I'm here. Take it easy. Don't be afraid." He stood there, keeping an eye on her, encouraging her, protecting her, letting her rest. After 20 minutes or so, she struggled to her feet. Her partner began to chirp loudly and excitedly. "You can do it! You can do it! You can do it!" he chirped (or so it seemed to me!). And she did! She flew off, and he went after her as they disappeared down the street.

It was such a little drama, with such tiny actors, but what a big truth. The little lady finch may have been just fine all by herself. Maybe a cat would not have come along. Maybe she did not need her friend to help her get on her feet again. But God gave her friends and protectors to encourage and pray for her. He will do the same for you and me.

He does care for the little sparrow (and goldfinches!) as He cares for all His creatures, great and small. So the next time you go flying hard into that glass door, whether it is sorrow, pain, worry, failure, grief, or worse, remember that He will make sure someone prays for you. He will put you in a safe place. He will send someone to encourage you. And He will give you wings to fly high once again.

4
God's Strength in Our Weakness

Scripture tells us we were created in the image of God, but often when we look in the mirror, we realize that image falls mighty short. Sometimes it is a matter of birth. Sometimes we have been the victim of violence or an accident. And sometimes we have chosen unwisely and our choices have exacted their toll.

Psalm 34:18 is a passage that brings me great comfort when I am facing health issues of my own. *"The LORD is close to the broken-hearted and saves those who are crushed in spirit."* There will be times when our hearts are broken and we feel crushed because of physical ailments. When we take these problems to the Lord and honestly tell Him how we feel, we can be certain He is nearby. If God does not immediately take away our pain, suffering, or disabilities, we can be sure He is using them for an important reason. Sometimes God's greatest work is revealed through the difficulties He allows us to face.

Whatever the reason, though, when we don't look "normal" or feel "normal," it is hard to remember we are beautiful and loved in His eyes. God does not make mistakes and has a plan for each of us. Psalm 139 reminds us we are "fearfully and wonderfully made" and that God's thoughts of us are precious. So why do we go through such difficult times and situations? Only He knows for sure. Perhaps it is so we can be Jesus' arms of comfort and encouragement to those who have yet to discover His grace.

> *Are any among you suffering? They should pray. Are any cheerful? They should sing songs of praise. Are any among you sick? They should call for the elders of the church and have them pray over them, anointing them with oil in the name of the Lord* (James 5:13-14 NRSV).

> It was not Spain and this was not a dream. A raging bull was
> coming at him full steam, and Kevin could not outrun him. My
> husband was not prepared for the physical aftermath of this
> life-threatening attack, but he was prepared to meet his Maker.
> From the moment of impact until he walked out of the hos-
> pital one month later, Kevin put the power of prayer to work.
> We never know when God will call us home, and it is impor-
> tant to know where we plan to spend eternity.

Bull Attack

BY KEVIN BOTTKE, FARIBAULT, MINNESOTA

It was a beautiful fall day, and the three of us were just completing
the finishing touches on a newly constructed hay feeder. With pas-
tures short and winter in the air, our herd of beef cattle lingered around
the feeder, instinctively knowing that grazing was over for the season
and food would now come from this area. Five-month-old calves ran
playfully around the barnyard, under the watchful eyes of their
mothers. Hereford cattle are a docile breed, and I had grown up around
them. Our children were active in 4-H, having won many awards
for showing these gentle giants. We were no strangers to handling
cattle, including the care and feeding of the daddy of our herd, Aaron.

Aaron was a nearly 2000-pound hunk of muscle. With horns that
spanned a good three feet or more from tip to tip, we had had him
since he was just over a year old. At four, he was coming into his
own and strutted around his family that day, watching—waiting.

My son, Kermit, was operating the skid loader—a noisy con-
traption that made it difficult for those within earshot to hear themselves think, let alone carry on a conversation. Our hired hand, Matt,
was using electric hand tools on the feed bunk, adding more noise

to the mix. I was walking across the pasture toward the barn, in the middle of an open area, when out of the corner of my eye I saw unusually fast movement.

My blood ran cold as I looked over my shoulder. Charging full speed was Aaron, the bull—coming right for me. Taking off like an Olympic runner when the starting gun shoots, I knew I would be a goner if I did not get away.

"Kermit!" I shouted as I ran.

But no one could hear me over the din of equipment.

No match for a full-steam, raging bull on attack, I knew I was not going to make it to safety.

"God, help me!" I yelled just as Aaron's powerful head rammed me in the back, sending me flying into the air and crashing back to earth with a thud that put out my lights for the next several minutes—the first of many blessings I was to experience. I would not want to have been conscious for what happened next.

A raging bull has one focus and one focus only: to take the life from its target. It uses its powerful head as a battering ram, its hooves as a method to roll around its prey, and its horns to protect itself. There is little a human being can do when under its capture. Most of us have seen news clips of rodeo accidents or bullfighting in Spain. Few people survive a full-on bull attack.

The moment I landed on the ground, Aaron rammed, stomped, and beat on me, rolling me about 40 feet from that open area of pasture into the cement base of our corncrib. At that point, with nowhere else to go, the ramming began in earnest. I was going down for the count.

Suddenly the beating stopped. Motionless, I began to regain consciousness as I heard the roar of the skid loader and looked up to see the machine nearly on top of me.

Hearing none of the savage snorting of the raging bull, at some point during the attack Kermit had looked up to see me being rolled into the base of the corncrib. Thinking fast, he roared into action.

As Aaron came in for the kill, Kermit rammed the bull with the bucket of the skid loader several times, diverting the bull's attention from me. My son's quick thinking saved my life, as Aaron retreated to lick his own wounds.

"Get the cell phone! Call 911!" I heard my son yell to Matt.

"Where is it? I can't find it!" Matt yelled back.

Watching them frantically looking for the phone as they kept an eye on the bull and took in my mashed and battered body, I vividly recall feeling *their* pain as they looked in horror at me and thought I surely must be dead.

"Thank You, God. Thank You, God. Thank You, God," I said over and over in my mind, willing my eyes to open and my mouth to speak.

"Dad! Dad!" Kermit cried out.

"The ambulance is on its way. They're coming. Can you hear me? Dad?"

I began to see, hear, and think. But I could not talk. I could not move.

My macho instinct was to get up, dust myself off, and march onward like a good Christian soldier. But God had other plans.

Kermit will tell you today that he was praying to God from the moment he looked up and saw me under the bull's massive head. How he thanked God when I began to speak, because he thought for sure I was gone.

"Darn bull," I said. "Give him a bullet," I mumbled and tried to smile.

This phrase we jokingly used around the barnyard any time a critter of any shape or size caused trouble—"give him a bullet"— was more a joke than anything. But this time I sensed Kermit would quickly have done just that if a gun had been nearby.

It was a good sign that I wasn't paralyzed. Then I began slowly to *feel*, as well. Let me tell you, that is when I knew I was in big trouble, 'cause the pain was beyond comprehension. And something told me it was going to get worse before it got better.

"Oh God, oh God." My moans went from my mouth to His ears. "Stay calm, Kevin. Focus, Kevin. I'm here. I'm here." The peace and comfort of God enveloped me. I felt His presence.

Suddenly it seemed as though half the town had arrived: the ambulance and paramedic team, the fire department rescue squad, several sheriff deputies, and even neighbors, all making quite a commotion. We live in a small town of less than 21,000, and many folks had heard on their police-band scanners that a bull had attacked Kevin Bottke on his farm property out by Roberds Lake. Those close by had come to see how they could help.

"Hey, Kevin, keep your day job. You're a lousy bullfighter," a neighbor joked, trying to take my mind off the situation.

Unbeknownst to me, I looked quite the sight. Covered in blood, mud-caked, bruised, and battered, I had begun to swell. My left leg was turned at an inhuman angle, and because the horns of the bull were so menacing, it was a general consensus I must have been gored. I may have been alive, but the clock was ticking, and the professionals on the scene felt I was most likely not going to make it. Most victims of bull attacks like mine don't.

I recall someone using some type of power scissors, cutting off my boots and some of my clothing.

"No visible puncture wounds," I heard.

"Thank You, God," I said.

"Internal bleeding probable," someone added.

"If that's so…God please help me now," I prayed.

Things were happening quickly all around me, yet my sole focus was on praying and willing my left leg to move, but it would not. I couldn't bring myself to look down. In fact, I am not sure I could have moved my head if I had tried. I didn't want to see the area of my body that to me seemed the most damaged.

After a quick assessment of my injuries, I was secured on a stretcher, moved into the ambulance, and taken to our local hospital—

my first stop before being transported to St. Mary's Mayo Medical Center Trauma Unit in Rochester. As a Christian, I had come to know the Lord as my Savior as a very young boy. Prayer was an important part of my life, yet never before had my petitions to the Lord been so personal. I wanted to communicate with my family and with the attendants, but the majority of my communication was going on in my head as I talked nonstop to God.

Over the course of the next minutes, hours, days, weeks, and months, the amazing power of prayer not only comforted me, but also brought miraculous occurrences every step of the way. I could visibly see God's hand at work, and my faith grew stronger as my body slowly followed suit.

God moved friends and family to come to the hospital and pray around my bedside as physicians prepped me for surgery. He brought me the finest medical team at just the right time to save me as a potentially life-threatening swelling syndrome brought on by the brutal attack began to shut down my heart.

It was by God's grace alone that I had no internal bleeding, that the bull's massive horns did not puncture any vital organs, and that for all intents and purposes I was alive. The majority of the damage was to my left tibia—it had been pulverized beyond belief. When told I would be better off in the long run if I granted permission for my leg to be amputated, I prayed again to God.

"Lord, You gave me this body and You've brought me this far. Please help me keep all my parts, okay?"

And He did.

It took five surgeries, skin grafting, wearing painful equipment literally screwed into my leg for over one year, and enduring countless hours of therapy to keep my leg.

Today I walk with a slight limp and require a special lift in my shoe because my left leg is shorter than my right—a small price to pay for keeping life and limb.

My son was awarded a special Congressional commendation for his heroic actions, and even though I am primarily known as a real estate broker, some folks still introduce me as Faribault's premiere bullfighter. My collection of bull memorabilia has few rivals in the area.

When my wife asked me to write about how God answered my prayers during this ordeal, it was difficult to know where to begin.

From the moment Kermit looked up to see the bull rolling me in the dirt to today, seven years later, I can clearly see the hand of God in my life. And at the very core of it all is prayer.

My prayers and the intercessory prayers of countless loved ones are responsible not only for my life today, but for the *quality* of my life today. Many people have traumatic, life-changing accidents. The fact mine was so dramatic and unique for a midwestern farm guy might add some flare to the retelling of the tale, but the bottom line when all is said and done is that prayer changes things—if we let it.

Prayer changed how I viewed my circumstances, my pain, my options, my blessings, and my future. Prayer gave me legs to walk when my own legs would not carry me. Every time God answered one of my prayers, from the small ones to the major ones, my faith increased with the knowledge that I was never alone—not for a minute.

I was a pretty average kind of guy, who had lived a pretty average kind of life, until God used a less-than-average kind of accident to teach me a powerful lesson.

I had been praying all my life, but had failed to really see the blessings of answered prayer all around me: the blessings of children who love the Lord, the blessings of a wife who dropped everything to nurture me back to health, the blessings of family and friends who had often prayed with me and for me even before the bull attack, and the blessings of having a forgiving God who sent His own Son to die a painful death for me so that I might live as a free man.

Yes, my life was changed that day. God answered my prayers from the moment I looked over my shoulder to see the charging bull, until this very moment when I recall the attack. But more important, He made me see that He had always been answering my prayers. I just had not taken the time to rest in His care and comfort long enough to see it.

> Have you ever felt the hand of God place itself upon your heart? Have you felt there is something very important He wants you to do? Delores prayed to find out exactly what the Lord wanted her to do and for Him to give her the courage to do it. It was an action she would never regret.

Strangers No More

BY DELORES CHRISTIAN LIESNER, RACINE, WISCONSIN

I was a relatively new teacher in a large urban high school and knew little about Richard, one of my fellow instructors, except that, at six foot four inches and with a bright smile, this active teacher was liked by everyone at the school.

But word was out that Richard had suffered a sudden heart attack and might have to limit his activities for the rest of the just-beginning school year. Everyone said it would be especially difficult for him. He was looking forward to bringing the senior class to commencement at the end of the year. He had worked with these young people for four years, bringing them through the throes of their freshmen, sophomore, and junior years. Now they were seniors, and Richard wanted to be part of their final year.

I turned curiously from stuffing mailboxes as I heard my boss greet Richard, who was pale from his recent heart surgery. I was alarmed at his unusual lack of spirit when Richard confirmed that his doctor had ordered immediate retirement. Although I barely knew him, I felt compelled to connect with him and called out casually, "Richard, I'll be praying for you."

Turning in the doorway, he met my gaze. "Thanks," he drawled slowly, "but I feel like my life is over. If I can't be with the students, what do I have to live for?" And he turned and walked out of the building.

I was stunned by his words and shocked that he would share such desperate thoughts with someone he barely knew. His words "my life is over" rang over and over in my mind. I was indeed going to pray for him, but now I considered that I might be called to do more than just pray. At once I thought, *Oh God, if I'm supposed to say something else to this hurting man I barely know, You're going to have to make it clear to me. But I'm willing, if that's what You want.*

As Thanksgiving vacation neared, my prayerful concern for Richard heightened. Uncomfortable about phoning someone I barely knew, I approached the school psychologist and my boss and urged *them* to call Richard, but both of them returned the burden to me.

"I know you have a strong feeling about Richard's situation, and I'd like you to call him," my boss said. He then offered to guard my closed office door to offer me the privacy I would need for such a conversation. I took him up on the offer.

"Hello?" Richard answered the phone himself.

"May I speak with your wife?" I asked nervously.

"She's not available currently." His voice carried the same melancholy tone I had heard when he spoke to my boss earlier that week. "She's busy with the kids getting packed for their trip to visit family, so she really can't talk right now."

"Okay. I'll call back later." I hung up the phone, disgusted with myself.

My heart clenched in fear as I recalled his words "packed for their trip." He was implying he was not going with them.

"Lord, should I call back? I have this feeling I should, but only if it's what You want." The urgency would not leave, and frantically I prayed that God would remove my fear and inhibitions, while I was redialing the number.

A phrase from a verse in the Bible came to mind—something about how when we give to others, at the same time we give to Him. Richard answered the phone again. "Hello?"

At that moment, a long-buried emotion released a flood of memories regarding a deep depression my dad had encountered following a heart attack. "Richard," I confessed, "I called a moment ago and asked to speak to your wife, because I didn't know if you would want to talk to me. I know we barely know one another, but your reaction to your surgery reminded me of my daddy, and I'd like to talk to you about him, if you don't mind."

His soft-spoken response that I should go ahead opened the door. "My dad loved his job and made it his life, until a sudden heart attack weakened him, both physically and emotionally. I remember one time he told me that he felt he'd never be whole again."

"I feel the same way," Richard admitted. "Is that what he said? Like he didn't feel whole? In those words?"

"Yes," I answered, and took his questioning as an invitation to continue. Memories of how our family felt flooded my mind, and I shared with Richard everything I remembered about that hard time in my life. I told him how helpless we all felt, unable to unlock the hold of depression on my dad. "He seemed beyond our reach, Richard. And we all felt like failures because we couldn't get through to him."

"I never thought that my family might be feeling that way." Richard opened up and shared that his family had been struggling to help him.

I explained how my seven-year-old son wrote John 3:16 on a card and carefully printed that he could trust God to love him even more than we could, because He gave His Son for us. "Once Dad found hope in God's message, he was ready to listen to the doctor's instructions. The doctor told him that depression was a common side effect for many people after heart surgery and nothing to be ashamed of."

"Really?" Richard's voice held a bit more life than before.

"Richard, will you do something for yourself?" I went on to ask him if he would make a few promises to me. "I want you to join your family trip for Thanksgiving. And while you're traveling with them, I'm going to ask you to write down everything that you know God has done for you and everything you learn from Him while you're away. Then when you come back, I'd like you to call your doctor and me."

After his assurances that he would call me after his vacation, we ended our conversation and I hung up my phone.

I opened the door to my office and looked up at my boss.

"Well, tell me how it went," he said.

"I made him promise to go on his family Thanksgiving trip and to call both the doctor and me when he arrived back in town."

I continued praying through the long weekend. When the holidays were over, I received a call from Richard. "You were absolutely right," he said. "The doctor told me I'm suffering from a side effect from surgery. He ordered a prescription for me today." He paused a moment and then added, "The other prescription you gave me—it changed my life."

But this is not the end of the story.

I received a card in the mail from one of Richard's daughters, saying, "I don't know what you shared with Dad, but whatever it was, it changed his life. We have our daddy back."

The next morning, a familiar shadow filled the doorway at work. I looked up from my desk to see a more healthy and peaceful-looking man. Richard was smiling. He queried the principal, "Did you know about her phone call?"

The principal nodded.

"Well, what she didn't know was that I had a gun ready with plans to use it that night. It took a phone call from a stranger to wake me up."

All three of us locked into a moment of startled silence and reverence for God's intervention. It was the six words that came next that put his words into perspective.

"But we are strangers no more."

"Am I only a God nearby," declares the LORD, "and not a God far away?" (Jeremiah 23:23). Emory and Carol knew He was not. When Emory was diagnosed with cancer and given very little time left, they knew prayer was the only way. Prayer was the tie that bound them together and gave them hope.

My Wife's Answered Prayer

BY EMORY G. MAY, SUVA, FIJI ISLANDS

It was 1987, and our family moved to a small town in eastern Montana where we would be ministering to an equally small congregation. My wife and I had been in the ministry for over 30 years, and we were excited about the opportunity of serving another church.

Later that year my mother, who lives in Florida, fell and broke her neck. My wife and I drove from Montana to spend a week with her while she recuperated. On our journey back home, my legs began to swell, and my feet felt as though I was walking on cut glass.

When we got home, I immediately went to my doctor. He told me, "Emory, it looks as though you ate too much fast food on the road. That stuff is filled with salt and often causes some people's legs to swell."

But the problem continued to get worse.

I passed out in church on a Sunday night, and my wife drove me 240 miles to a hospital in Billings, Montana. They examined me and told me I had a rare condition causing the symptoms I was experiencing. There was nothing they could do that could not be done at my local hospital, so they sent me back home.

Someone in our church mentioned that since I was a veteran, I could go to the VA hospital in Miles City, Montana. I called and set up an appointment. They immediately hospitalized me. That was two days before my forty-ninth birthday. The day following my birthday, they ran a CT scan and found what they identified as a blood clot, located in the pulmonary artery of my left lung. After several more tests, I was told that I had a malignant tumor in my left lung. It was inoperable, and they sent me to the VA hospital in Salt Lake City for further tests.

"I'm sorry, Emory, but if you see another Christmas, it will be a miracle." My doctor shared the news with compassion, but he told me exactly how it was.

Carol shared her thoughts with me later. "I truly thought that when I returned from Salt Lake City, you would be in a casket in the cargo hold of the airplane."

A church in Salt Lake City made arrangements for Carol to have a place to stay and provided her with a car. It turned out that the couple she was staying with were both nurses at the hospital, so they were privy to all of the test results—none of which were good.

When she visited me, Carol told me about their hospitality. "In the rush of leaving Montana, I forgot my Bible, so I asked if I could borrow one from them. They loaned me an old, well-worn Bible that belonged to the man's grandfather, a preacher." Tears poured from her eyes as she told me about her prayers: "Where are You, God, and why are these things happening?"

Then she told me about something that she had seen me do while searching for a word from God. She placed the Bible on the spine and let it fall open. "The Scripture leapt off the page, Emory. I read it several times: 'Am I only a God nearby,' declares the LORD, 'and not a God far away?' (Jeremiah 23:23)."

Carol told me that she went immediately to her knees in her attic room and asked God to lead, and that His will be done. "Please, Lord, just give us the courage and strength to go through whatever is ahead."

Test after test only showed the same conclusion. There were too many tumors to hope for survival. They covered my heart and both lungs. My left lung had completely collapsed, and there was no way to do surgery. Any treatment they considered was quickly dismissed as ineffective in my case.

Two weeks into my stay, to everyone's amazement, I started improving. When I entered the hospital, I couldn't walk the length of the bed, but now I could walk almost the length of the hospital. One day, 14 doctors walked into the room, pulled the curtain around my bed, and the chief medical officer said, "Mr. May, we don't know what has happened, but your tumors are gone."

My reply was quick and to the point: "Well then, I guess God healed me!"

The doctor was not so easily persuaded. "Well, if He did, we have no medical evidence of it. We're going to send you home, and when it returns, we'll deal with it." Even after all the CT scans, MRI's and biopsies, they were still not convinced.

The next day we were on an airplane headed home to Montana, where we spent the next three years in ministry. It has now been 17 years since my healing. Seldom a day goes by when I am not reminded of what our family endured during those months.

My complete recovery did not occur overnight, and it took me several months of rest and recuperation. But in April the following year, our son and I climbed a mountain in Waterton Lakes, Alberta.

It was a simple hiking trail and took us a while, but we have the pictures to prove it.

Jeremiah 23:23 still lives for Carol. She has shared it on a number of occasions. Is God a God afar off? No! He is a God who is with us during the storms of life.

I spent over ten years dealing with the sick and dying following my experience. I felt like I could minister to them, because I had been where they were.

There has seldom been a day that I have not shared the love and power of God to heal. Sometimes He does, and sometimes He doesn't, but at all times He can.

To be honest, I never did ask God to heal me. I remember my request: "God, I have *told* Your people for over 30 years how to die. Now let me *show* them." The prayers for healing came from my wife, and I will be forever thankful for her prayers and her faith.

Cancer...the most dreaded word that could be spoken by our physician. Many times upon hearing it, loved ones lose hope and grow in despair. Suzanne and Richard knew they could not give up. Together they prayed for God to come to Suzanne's rescue. They did not know "the rest of the story," but God did.

The Rest of the Story

BY T. SUZANNE ELLER, MUSKOGEE, OKLAHOMA

It was simply a routine checkup, nothing out of the ordinary... "except for that small lump," I told the doctor casually, like telling my hairdresser that I needed a trim.

I wasn't worried. After all, I was only 32 years old. I was healthy. The word *cancer* never occurred to me.

Before the week was out, I was immersed in a world where every sentence began with *cancer*.

Not only did I have breast cancer, but it had spread to my lymph nodes. I was rolled from room to room, each with a new set of needles and tests. One test revealed an ominous shadow on my brain. That night the doctors filed into my hospital room.

The shadow seemed to be cancerous. If it were, the stats of surviving five years had just spiraled downward from 40 percent to 10 percent—that is, after radical surgery, chemotherapy, and radiation. When the doctors left the room, my husband and I sat wrapped in our grief. My children were all under the age of nine. I was married to the man I loved, and we had lots of plans for the future.

The doctors were not able to promise that I would emerge unscathed from surgery, if it was needed. The shadow loomed over my central vortex—home to my memory, sight, and personality.

I closed my eyes, and suddenly these words began to wash over me: "But we have this treasure in jars of clay to show that this all-surpassing power is from God and not from us. We are hard pressed on every side, but not crushed; perplexed, but not in despair; persecuted, but not abandoned; struck down, but not destroyed."

The words were from my worn Bible, but the soft, cracked, determined voice was that of my husband, Richard. As he read, the words of 1 Corinthians 4:7-9 penetrated my heart.

God was in control, no matter where He chose to take me on this journey. He would mold me and shape me and be with me during this difficult time. I was a jar of clay in the Potter's hands.

I did not know the "rest of the story," but God did. However it turned out, I was in His hands.

Peace filled our room—peace more powerful than the cancer. We praised God, singing softly and sharing in the presence of God.

Nurses came in and tiptoed back out, aware of the news we had received, but amazed at the calm that lingered over us.

The next morning they wheeled me down the hall. It was time to get a clearer picture of the findings from the day before. "It will only take 30 minutes," they said. Two hours later, I was still confined in the metal tube. My husband was in the room with me. His only contact point was my bare feet sticking out of the tube. He rubbed my feet and prayed as the whirring MRI took pictures of my brain.

Hours later, I was surrounded by my family and friends. I was on the phone with my nine-year-old daughter when my doctor rushed in, still in his street clothes.

"It was clear!" he shouted. "It's gone."

My husband slid down the wall and started weeping. My mother-in-law ran out of the room, celebrating. My pastor leaped in the air. I sat stunned by the news.

It was the first of many miracles over the next year.

I gently fought against my loving family, believing that if God performed this miracle on my head, I did not need further treatment for what was happening to the rest of my body.

"You've had cancerous tumors removed from your lymph nodes and chest. Please get the rest of the treatments—please." They were frightened, and in the end, they won.

I sat in the vinyl chair, waiting for the nurse to slip the needle in my vein. "Give them peace," I prayed. "Let them know You are with each of us in this battle." I had fought through the frustration, even anger, at having to sit in that chair, in that room, with a needle in my hand.

The nurse gave me a sheaf of papers listing scary side effects: nausea, hair loss, weakness. The list went on. Later that day I stood in front of the mirror. My skin was pale, see-through. The veins in my chest and arms looked like slender blue rope.

But I was not sick.

For the next nine months I went through chemotherapy and radiation. Instead of losing weight, I gained over 20 pounds. Many times I left the office with my hand wrapped in gauze and went to play volleyball with the teen ministry at my church. Each week I sat in the chair. My long, curly hair reached below my shoulders—a tangible reminder that the Potter was in control.

One day the doctor's office called. My white count had crashed, and my immune system was dangerously low. "Leave work," they said. "Make sure that you stay away from anyone with a cold or the flu."

My children climbed off the school bus later that day. I watched them straggle up the sidewalk, their faces flushed, their eyes heavy. I rocked, bathed, and ministered to my children as they wrestled with high fevers. When my husband came home, he took over. But hours later he, too, was sick and running a high fever. I took care of my family for the next three days and was never sick.

As the years have passed, I have celebrated each small and large victory. But I have also asked God that I not waste the gift I have been given. I realize that I have been given a second chance to live life.

On the fifth anniversary of the discovery of my cancer, I left the corporate world and ran after my passion in writing and ministry. I decided life is not about money, but about doing what God wants.

On my tenth anniversary, I went on a rugged missions trip to the Amazon in Brazil, sleeping on a hammock and working in a clinic during the day. Life is not about comfort or things, and yet I feel rich as I put a pair of glasses on the face of someone who could not see moments before.

This year on my thirteenth anniversary, I will celebrate a quarter of a century with the love of my life.

"When will you decide that I am cured?" I asked my doctor one day, grinning.

"You were out of my hands a long time ago," he said.

It's true. But only God knows what is ahead. I just ask that He continue to shape and mold this fragile jar of clay as He spins out "the rest of the story."

❧ ❧ ❧

When having a child seems the most important event in a marriage, finding out you probably will never have one of your own can be earthshaking. Through prayer God can orchestrate miraculous happenings in our lives. John and Pat knew this and were faithful in their prayers. *"In all your ways acknowledge him, and he will make your paths straight"* (Proverbs 3:6). And God answered in an unexpected manner!

Not Impossible with God

BY P. JEANNE DAVIS, PHILADELPHIA, PENNSYLVANIA

The gynecologist's news was not what I wanted to hear.

"It's not utterly impossible, but it's extremely improbable you'll ever become pregnant." After multiple surgeries for a chronic condition called endometriosis, her words did not come as a surprise. I knew my chances of conceiving were slim, and my age further complicated matters. I was well into my forties. My doctor handed my husband some information on an upcoming adoption seminar. "You might want to consider adoption."

After months of consideration, John and I retained an attorney who specialized in private, independent adoption. We were very enthusiastic about our choice and ready to become parents.

"I know there's a child out there for us," I told my husband.

One and a half years passed by without a word; nevertheless, we remained determined and hopeful. My husband and I leaned heavily on God's promise: "In all your ways acknowledge him, and he will make your paths straight" (Proverbs 3:6).

I decided to contact the doctor who first suggested adoption to us. I wasn't sure what help she could be exactly, but was determined to pursue every possible avenue. Her encouragement had been a crucial factor in our decision to begin the adoption process, and I felt I needed to touch base with her again.

"She's been relocated," the receptionist told me. "She's taken her practice to another city."

"Can I have her new number?" I reached for a pen. The receptionist rattled off the number, and I quickly scribbled it down. "Thank you so much."

"May I speak to Dr. Reed, please?"

"She's currently with a patient. May I take a message, or would you like to speak with the nurse practitioner?" I could hear Dr. Reed's familiar music playing faintly in the background.

"I'll go ahead and leave a message, if that's okay." I gave her my name and asked her to have the doctor call me as soon as she could.

When she returned my call, I could tell she was surprised to hear from me. "Jeanne? This is Dr. Reed. How are you? Are you in town?"

"No, I'm not, but I felt I needed to talk to you," I replied. "Do you remember when my husband and I spoke with you briefly about adoption?"

"Yes, I do. Are you calling to tell me you have a baby?"

"Unfortunately, no. We've been through all the red tape and completed all the requirements for a private adoption, but it's been over a year and we still don't have a child." Tears were building in my eyes. I was desperate. "Does it usually take this long?"

"Sometimes it takes longer, Jeanne, but I'm going to keep your number and call you if something comes up on this end. I'm sorry you've had to wait so long already."

Her voice comforted me somehow, but I knew she needed to get back to her patients, so I thanked her and said good-bye.

Before she hung up, she said, "Jeanne, it will happen. It just takes time—sometimes a lot of time. Keep me updated, okay?"

I told her I would and then hung up with one thought: *I wonder how much time.*

The answer came ten days later. When we started the adoption process, we had a second line installed so we would not miss phone calls. The phone rang, and I silently prayed as I went to the phone.

The caller surprised me. It was Dr. Reed. But what she said next surprised me even more. "You're not going to believe this, but I have a baby for you."

I was too excited to say anything, and my heart was leaping in my chest.

She continued to explain. "The same afternoon you called my office, a mother came in with her teenage daughter. We ran a pregnancy test, and it came back positive."

I had to sit down.

"This young mother knows she's unable to care for a baby, so she's made the decision to give it up for adoption. I told her about you and John. She wants a Christian home for her baby, and I assured her that you and John had been praying for a child for many years. She'd like to meet you both." Dr. Reed was clearly amazed. "The timing of your call the other day was a remarkable coincidence."

I knew a better explanation. God's hand had orchestrated this whole thing. He was the One who prompted me to call Dr. Reed that day, not the long arm of coincidence. I knew immediately that this baby belonged to us.

"The birth mother's requests are these: 'Give the child a loving, nurturing home and lots of love,' " Dr. Reed had explained.

I assured her we would do exactly that.

Nearly eight months later, on an overcast spring morning, John and I were awakened by "the" phone call.

"It's a boy—and he's beautiful!" Dr. Reed announced.

John and I couldn't get to the hospital fast enough. Dr. Reed was waiting for us in the nursery. She walked over to a bassinet, lifted out our son, and brought him close to the window so we could see his tiny features. She nodded at the nurse, who brought us each a sterile gown. We washed our hands and were escorted to the other side of the window. I was first to hold him.

"My son," I murmured, pulling him close. He was beautiful. John wrapped his arms around us both. We were so grateful to God and to the young woman who gave us her son.

Three short days later, we brought our baby home. Our family was complete. We named our newborn son Johnny.

One year later, I became ill and could not shake the nausea. I considered the chance I might be pregnant. Impossible! I was 48 years old and infertile. But I wasn't getting better. I had to tell my husband. "John, I think I might be, uh, I mean, I think I'm pregnant." Even as I said it, I found it impossible to believe.

He looked at me skeptically, but decided we had better visit the doctor quickly.

We did see the doctor and heard the words I had forever given up on: "Your pregnancy test is positive." My doctor was as surprised as I was.

"I can't believe it!" John and I said in unison as we clung to each other in utter shock and joy. "How will we cope with two babies at our age? Aren't I too old? Will the baby be healthy?"

The doctor assured me that she would do all she could to see that we had a positive outcome. Eight months later after a healthy pregnancy, Joshua, who tried to come into the world upside down, made his appearance via cesarean section.

"This is truly a miracle baby!" My obstetrician was thrilled. "One for the records, for sure. Just your age alone makes it extraordinary."

Soon after Joshua's birth, I wrote to Dr. Reed, explaining to her that John and I had a new addition to our family.

A few months later while talking with her over the telephone, it became apparent she had misunderstood my letter. "You've adopted another child, right?"

When I explained that I had just given birth to our new son, she could not believe it. "Impossible!" Her reaction hardly contained the happiness in her voice.

Today Johnny and Joshua are in elementary school. When days are rough with the busy demands of parenting, I remember how God responded to the desire of our hearts in miraculous ways. I know first-hand that "all things are possible with God"!

5
God at the Hour of Death

Mark 5:36 records Jesus as saying, "Don't be afraid; just believe." Should we fear death and dying? No, not if we know the Lord. It is a fact that one day we will all leave this world. We will stand before God, and He will ask us a very important question: "What did you do with My Son?" How will we respond? The answer will determine where we will spend our future. Time here on earth is like a second compared to the amount of time we will spend in eternity. We should not fear dying. Our greatest fear should be in not living. And the only way to live life to its fullest is to live it in Christ. We need to pray for God's guidance and allow Him to show us how to prepare for our future with Him.

Listen, I will tell you a mystery: We will not all sleep, but we will all be changed—in a flash, in the twinkling of an eye, at the last trumpet. For the trumpet will sound, the dead will be raised imperishable, and we will be changed. For the perishable must clothe itself with the imperishable, and the mortal with immortality. When the perishable body has been clothed with the imperishable, and the mortal with immortality, then the saying that is written will come true: "Death has been swallowed up in victory." "Where, O death, is your victory? Where, O death, is your sting?" The sting of death is sin, and the power of sin is the law. But thanks be to God! He gives us the victory through our Lord Jesus Christ (1 Corinthians 15:51-57).

Almost every one of us will someday face the loss of a parent. Still, as the days draw short, we pray for more. We pray for one more Christmas, one more birthday, one more chance to laugh and remember simpler times. Slowly, suddenly, the answer becomes clear. Prayer, like our heavenly Father, is eternal. And, as Michael learns, the answered prayer of a mother resides in the lives of her children.

With Sighs Too Deep for Words

BY MICHAEL DANDRIDGE, TEMPLE, TEXAS

"I can't find God."

"It's okay, Mom." I try to sound confident and strong.

"No, it's not!" She clutches my arms and strains to rise out of her bed. "It's not okay! I'm dying, and I can't find God!"

Her words terrify me. She has never said anything about dying before. I pretend otherwise, but I, too, am afraid. I have doubts of my own, and if my mom, nearing death, cannot find God…well then, maybe He simply isn't there.

"You'll find Him, Mama. It will be okay. You'll find Him."

"Promise?" Now she sounds like a child asking for a puppy, and I recognize the voice. It is my voice as a child.

When I was six or seven, I remember a fly landing on my mom's hamburger. When she shooed it away and started to take another bite, I said, "Ooh! Are you going to eat where that fly landed, Mama?"

She shrugged. "It's nothing. Probably just dropped off some cancer germs."

It seemed a strange thing to say. Even at that age, I sensed that she was kidding. Somehow I knew that flies did not carry "cancer germs," but why did she choose that disease? Why not malaria or dysentery or cooties? Was cancer on her mind, even then? I could not know that the calm surface of her casual remark concealed a deep pool of sadness and fear. It was years later I learned of her constant battle with clinical depression.

Our roles reversed, it is now my turn to reassure her that things are getting better, when it appears that things are getting worse. I wonder, *Was she as uncertain when making promises to me as I am now? Probably.*

"Promise?" she asks again.

I cannot force the words past the lump in my throat. I nod my head yes.

"Where are my people?"

"Your people?"

"Where are my people?" she repeats forcefully.

"Well, I'm right here, and Dad and the girls are in the next room..."

"My grandson! Where's Christopher?"

I run to the living room and grab my two-year-old son from in front of the television. He begins to whine in protest, and then becomes silent as I carry him into his grandmother's room. He senses something is wrong.

Mom's face brightens. "Hi, baby!"

Christopher speaks without my urging. "Hi, Grandma."

We sit beside my mom's bed while she coos nonsensical endearments to her grandson. After a few minutes, she drifts into unconsciousness. I sit beside her, Christopher in my lap, and listen to her ragged and strained breathing.

Silently, I stand up and start to carry him out of the room.

"Wait!"

I turn around and see Mom sitting up in bed, smiling, alert and lucid. She raises her arm with the palm of her hand facing us and says, "Is this a grandma waving bye-bye?"

The poignancy of her remark makes the hair stand up on the back of my neck. I look for Christopher's reaction. He smiles and imitates her wave with his small hand.

Her smile fades as she looks at me. "My book! You have to finish it!"

Her book. When I was growing up, my mom and I shared a love of books and writing. We would joke about someday writing a best-seller. We would take turns saying, "You know, when I write the Great American Novel, then you'll be sorry." Of course, it was really no joke. What writer doesn't have starry-eyed dreams of New York publishing houses and six-figure advances?

Then one day she decided to do something about her dreams. At the age of 35, Mom went back to college. At 40 she received her master's degree in Library Science. A few years later, she landed the job of her dreams. It was a routine physical for job placement that led to the discovery of her cancer. She began to write in earnest then, but it wasn't the Great American Novel. It was a journal of the last four years of her life—her "book."

I look for the manuscript in her study. Pages and pages of type-written text cover her desk. Next to her typewriter of choice, an old IBM Selectric, is a manila folder with a rubber band around it. Removing the rubber band, I open the folder to reveal the title page.

With Sighs Too Deep for Words
by Phyllis Dandridge

It was not fair. It was not fair that instead of writing a novel celebrating life, she was composing a chronicle of death. I remember the anger I felt when Mom first told us of her cancer. As a Christian, I knew just where to place that anger. What kind of God allows a woman to come within sight of her dreams, only to have them yanked out of reach?

At first, I prayed. I prayed for her healing, prayed for remission, prayed for a miracle. I read and heard all the stories of faith strengthened and renewed by recoveries that defied medical science. But it was not to be for my mother. Each doctor's visit brought more bad news. Somewhere during that time, I stopped praying. It didn't seem to make any difference.

Mom fought for every year she lived. Each year she survived was the result of sheer will and determination, and I did not see God's hand in any of it. And then two days ago, we got the call: *"Your mother only has a few days left, maybe just a few hours."*

Through hot tears, I turn the page and begin to read aloud to Mom from her book: "Each morning when I open my eyes to a new day, feelings of love and thanksgiving wash over me. I am still alive at the top of the mountain."

"I am still alive?"

I look up from her book.

"Please finish it!"

"I will."

"Why can't I find God? Why won't He answer my prayer? Where's God?" she cries.

"Mom…" I search for the words. I try to pray. It has been too long. I have forgotten how. Her question looms in my mind. *Where's God? Where's God? Where's God?*

Then I hear a voice answer her.

"Phyllis? Phyllis. Over here."

I turn to look for the source. There in the doorway stands a silhouette of a large entity in dark clothing. Now I don't believe that God makes house calls, so I am thinking this guy must be an angel. Yet Mom seems to recognize him.

"Hello," my mom answers.

He walks, or maybe he floats, into the room. He kneels beside my mother's bed and takes her hand.

"Phyllis, I'm Joshua Hall. Do you recognize me?"

"Yes. You're Father Hall from my church."

He smiles. "That's right. I came by to see how you're doing. Your husband tells me you have some concerns about God."

"Yes! Oh, yes! I can't find Him. I keep praying and praying, but I can't find God!" Her plea is heartrending.

Father Hall places his other hand over my mom's. "Phyllis, that's all right. You don't have to find God."

"Why not?"

"Because God can find you."

I am stunned at the power of that statement.

"Oh." She smiles and breathes a sigh of recognition. "Of course," she says. The tension leaves her face and, for the first time in days, her whole body relaxes into the bed. She closes her eyes. My mother has found peace.

After a few moments of silence, Father Hall speaks.

"Romans 8:26."

"What?" I ask.

"The verse." He points to my mom's manuscript lying on the nightstand: "In the same way, the Spirit helps us in our weakness. We do not know what we ought to pray for, but the Spirit himself intercedes for us with groans that words cannot express" (Romans 8:26).

"Oh. That's her journal. What does that verse mean, anyway?"

He looks at me and our eyes lock. "Have you ever tried to pray, but you just couldn't find the words? Maybe you were too tired or scared, or too angry at God?"

"Yeah. Right now."

"Understandable. Well, at times like this, the Holy Spirit prays for you. The Spirit prays in a language that cannot be expressed in words."

"I'm sure there were plenty of times when Mom was too angry and too tired to find the words. But she knew that the Holy Spirit would pray for her?"

"That's right."

"But what good did it do her? She didn't get the answer to any of her prayers."

"Are you sure? Do you know all of her prayers?"

"No, I guess I don't."

After Father Hall leaves, I pick up the loose manuscript, flip through the pages to the end, and read her last written words: "Surely, it is the remaining prayer of every mother that she did everything she could for her children, that she somehow taught them enough, gave them enough, loved them enough. That is my prayer. I pray it was enough."

I place the manuscript on the nightstand and focus on my mother. She is still sleeping, her breathing finally measured and peaceful. Holding her hand in mine, I whisper the answer to her prayer.

"It was enough, Mama. It was enough."

Prayer has long been used to bring comfort to the sick and to the dying. Bedside vigils and prayer groups have helped many a loved one make their last journey in peace and contentment. Sharon learned how much of an impact this made during one special visit.

Hands Around the Bed

BY SHARON M. KNUDSON, ST. PAUL, MINNESOTA

Martha greeted us at the door with a warm smile, but her eyes were puffy and sad. She had a scared look on her face and a hushed voice, not at all the vivacious Martha we had known the year before. She had called a few of us in hopes we could come and pray. Dennis, her husband, was suffering from a brain tumor.

I was startled when I entered the living room and saw him—emaciated and lying in a hospital bed. I followed my husband to his bedside and felt my knees go weak. Dennis had no hair and no dentures, and his cheeks were sunken into his face. His eyes, however, were as bright as ever, and his smile lit up the room.

Dennis and Martha, a retired couple, had been our enthusiastic hosts for a Bible study the year before. Dennis radiated with the love of God, enjoying his Bible and the study of prophecy. He smiled easily and winked at his dog, Toby, who was usually near his side. The sessions had been wonderful, and our group had grown close as we shared our lives with each other.

Now we met again after not seeing each other for several months. A bit queasy in the stomach, I took my place with the others around the hospital bed. Dennis smiled as he greeted each of us in turn and clasped our hands in his.

Our animated conversation was probably a bit too loud and cheerful, but it served to cover our shock and sorrow. As we chatted with Dennis, group members glanced at one another with silent horror on their faces. Dennis was very weak and frail. He had already had radiation for the brain tumor, but the prognosis was not good. He had been given three to four months to live.

Dan, our small-group leader, took charge in the same relaxed way he had led our studies the year before. His gentle, matter-of-fact manner was a comfort.

"What do you want us to sing, Dennis?" asked Dan.

"How Great Thou Art," was Dennis's instant reply.

And so we sang, and Dennis sang along. The music struck a deep chord within me and made me want to cry. Dan knew all the words, so it was easy for the rest of us to follow. When we had finished all three verses, Dennis chose "Great Is Thy Faithfulness" and then "Amazing Grace." He sang the melody and every word earnestly with a loud voice. It was exhausting for him, but he persevered through every hymn.

Then Dan read Psalms 37 and 23. Dennis beamed. He loved the Scriptures!

We closed with prayers, holding hands in a circle. Dennis, in his bed, was part of that circle, just as he had been the year before. We prayed for healing. We prayed that God would bless both Dennis and Martha in every way. We prayed for God's love and comfort to pour down on them. We closed with the Lord's Prayer, and again, Dennis joined in with a clear, strong voice.

Martha insisted that we have some refreshment and apologized that she had not baked anything. *Oh, my,* I thought, *how could she possibly think of dessert at a time like this?* I remembered how last year's gatherings had always concluded with her homemade delicacies: Dutch apple pie, strawberry shortcake, cinnamon rolls, oatmeal raisin cookies. She had taken many prizes at baking contests over the years and loved to treat us week after week. Now she served each of us a mere glass of soda through a profusion of grateful tears, shaking her head and wondering in whispers how much longer she might have Dennis with her. Only a few months, she was sure.

We stayed for only an hour, but sensed the presence of God in that home. Although I had been nervous about going there, I came away with peace in my heart. I had experienced the love and comfort of God, and it was evident that Dennis and Martha had, too.

Imagine our shock when we got a call the next morning saying Dennis had died peacefully in the night! Etched in my mind was the look on Dennis's face during the hymns and prayers. What a testimony his faith had been. In that brief hour, we had ministered to him, and he to us.

Then God had taken him to heaven—just like that!

No one knew that was to be Dennis's last evening on earth, that we would stand together so close to heaven's gates. But what a privilege we had been given, and thanks to a group leader who seemed to know what to do, we had handled ourselves well. In retrospect, we had held hands around Dennis's deathbed as we sang those hymns and prayed. It was an experience that I resolved to emulate if or when the opportunity ever presented itself again. Close-up, I had experienced the hand of God upon Dennis, and upon us all.

When Herman discovered his wife was losing her battle with cancer, he was unable to be at her side to offer comfort and help. Serving time in prison, he cried out to the Lord in anguish as his wife suffered alone. How God opened a door that seemed shut tight proved to Herman that God will not leave or forsake us, that God answers the deepest prayers of our heart.

God Is Good...All the Time

BY JAN ROADARMEL LEDFORD, FRANKLIN, NORTH CAROLINA
(AS TOLD BY HERMAN PARRAMORE)

The courtroom hushed to hear the verdict. My heart pounded in my throat.

The judge leaned over the bench and peered at me in obvious distaste. "This court finds you guilty. You are to report to the federal prison camp in Jesup, Georgia, where you will serve a 30-month term. Following your release..."

I barely heard him describe my three years' probation or the imposed fines. Thirty months in prison! Before this, the only trouble I had been in was a traffic violation...25 years ago!

But the judge wasn't through with me yet. "You should know something else," he continued with a frown. "I'd give you more time than this if I could. Unfortunately, 30 months is the most the law will allow."

It is not that I was being wrongfully imprisoned. I had owned a fertilizer manufacturing company in Tifton, Georgia, and had gotten into trouble over the storage of hazardous materials. We closed the plant, and the chemicals were cleaned up. While I had confessed my actions to the Lord and my church, I still had to face the consequences of what I had done. But I faced them knowing God had forgiven me. It was obvious that this judge had not.

So on December 5, 1995, I reported to the penal camp in Jesup, Georgia, to be processed as an inmate. That morning I kissed my wife, Delouise, good-bye and entered the facility. I do not remember ever being more frightened in my entire 60 years of life than I was when the gate slid between us and clicked shut. I prayed for Delouise just as much as I prayed for myself. Only God could help us through this.

The Jesup prison camp is unique, with no locked doors, no armed guards, no barbed wire. Your personal items are taken away. You are given clothing and a rule book, and are expected to comply. The prisoners stay in a dorm, which is a two-story cinder-block building. Instead of cells, two inmates share a "cube." The rooms are not actually walled off, but have partitions that stop before reaching the ceiling. Each cube has a doorway, but no door to close. As I was escorted to my cube, my prayers grew more frantic. "Lord, I don't know anyone. What will they do to a newcomer?"

I walked in to find a man in his late thirties sitting on one of the beds. He stood up when he saw me. "This is Les, your bunk mate," said the attendant. I was too frightened to offer my hand. I had been strictly warned never to touch anyone without that person's permission.

But Les stuck out his big, meaty palm. "Can I shake hands with you?" he asked. Then he indicated a couple of drawers on one end of a desk. "You can put your things in there."

"All I have are these clothes and my book," I said. For the first time in my life, I literally had nothing that was mine, not even a comb or toothbrush. Reality was sinking in like a millstone, settling in the pit of my stomach.

Les smiled a little. "Don't worry," he said. "Here, let me show you how they expect us to make our bunks."

Later that evening we were visited by several other prisoners. One of the men handed me a small plastic bag. "This is for you," he said. "It's a toilet kit with a toothbrush, soap, and stuff. It's from the Christian Brotherhood, a group of us inmates."

It was one of the best gifts I had ever been given.

The next night I eagerly attended Bible study with these same men. They had a sort of brotherhood greeting, what we would have called a responsive reading at church. One would say, "God is good!" and the others would respond, "All the time!"

Given the situation, I wondered sometimes how they could repeat the words so fervently. Being apart was tough on Delouise and me. I was allowed to phone her periodically, but prisoners cannot take calls except in an emergency. Delouise had to handle the sale of our home, a move into an apartment, and an increasingly painful back without me.

Late one April afternoon I was summoned to the case manager's office. I trudged downstairs, wondering what was going on. In his office with pale-green cinder-block walls, the case manager looked solemn. "You have a call from your stepdaughter," he said. My heart sank as I reached for the phone, thinking of Delouise's escalating problems with her back and a recent, unexplained weight gain...problems that she always glossed over.

"Herm?" My stepdaughter's voice was full of tears. "It's Mom." And all I could do was sit in that celery-colored room and listen as Sylvia told me that Delouise had been given a sentence of her own. She had cancer.

I don't remember going back to my cube after the phone call. But there I was, sitting on my properly made bed, pouring out my heart to God: "I've got to be with her somehow!" But I had not been there long enough, and I had too much time left to qualify for a furlough.

At that time, supporters on the outside began working for my early release. But I despaired when I learned that the final word on such a reprieve rested with none other than the same judge who had sentenced me. His angry words, "I'd give you more time if I could," kept repeating themselves in my mind.

Meanwhile, Delouise moved in with Sylvia and went through surgery and chemotherapy. At times she seemed much better and was able to visit me. My heart broke for her when her beautiful, strawberry-blonde hair fell out as a result of the chemo. But she wore a jaunty, colorful scarf on her head and laughed at me.

"When it grows back in, it'll be flaming orange," she joked, trying to cheer *me* up, when I should have been cheering *her* up.

By October, though, it was obvious that the chemotherapy was not working. The doctors said she had maybe two months to live. Requests for my early release had risen to the congressional level, without results. I was offered one four-day furlough—for bedside or graveside. I chose to go visit Delouise right away.

"Let's not talk about the bad things," she said in a weak voice as I held her hand. "Let's talk about the good things." So we did, expecting these were the last days we would spend together. They flew by quickly.

The night I returned to Jesup, I lay alone and sleepless on my bunk, facing the wall. At times I was consumed with guilt, knowing my own actions had gotten me here. God's goodness seemed far away.

The next day, I was again called to the case manager's office. I feared the worst, but he didn't say anything about a phone call. What he did say was astounding.

"What do you know about a release?" he asked me.

I was at a loss. "Nothing," I replied, "except that I want one!"

He indicated some papers on his desk. "I have a court order here for your release." The appeals of friends and family had finally gotten through, and somehow the judge had been convinced.

Tears began streaming down my face. "Praise the Lord!" I cried. And at 8:00 the next morning I left the prison a free man, by God's grace.

When I got to Sylvia's house, Delouise looked radiant. "I'd asked God to let me live long enough to see you set free," she confided. "I'd pretty much given up. God is so good!"

Five days after my release, Delouise was delivered, too. God sent an angel to open *her* prison door, and she flew away home. As I sat with my family at her funeral, I was grieving, but I was also rejoicing. The gift of those last five days together warmed my heart, and they still do today.

Yes, my fellow inmates were right. God is good. All the time!

There are times when God does not answer our prayers as we think He should—times when we tell Him what we want and He does not deliver. Yet it is often during those times of pain and despair when we cry out to God in anger that we come to understand that our prayers were, in fact, answered. We just had to be still and realize that sometimes no is an answer.

No Is an Answer

BY JUNE L. VARNUM, LOYALTON, CALIFORNIA

Why didn't God answer my prayers to heal my husband? Other prayers had been answered: comfort and return of my health following two miscarriages, successful recovery for my husband after open-heart surgery, safe return of four family members from three wars. Matthew 21:22 promises, "If you believe, you will receive whatever you ask for in prayer." I did believe. I *knew* my husband, Red, would be healed from malignant brain tumors.

After his death, the family went home and resumed their lives. But I was left with an empty life and a heart full of questions. Why didn't God heal Red? Why didn't He answer my prayers this time? Was it wrong to pray for healing? Didn't I have enough faith? I never prayed "Thy will be done." Was God angry that I didn't pray for His will to be done?

I ended up yelling at God, "You let him die. You didn't answer my prayers to heal him. You said no. Why didn't You answer my prayers?"

One morning, I forced myself to do some reorganizing. I opened the cabinet in our bathroom and reached for Red's medication bottles. Pulling off the cap of one bottle, I slowly dropped the capsules into the toilet. *You don't need these anymore,* I thought. I emptied a second and then a third bottle into the toilet. By the time I got to the fourth bottle, my vision was blurred. I hurled its contents into the toilet and wiped away the dampness on my cheeks. Our life, our marriage, was not supposed to end like this. I grew angry with God and began to doubt the need to pray and the power of prayer.

Two-and-a-half months earlier, I had returned home from grocery shopping. Red stood in the kitchen, rubbing his right hand and arm. He said they didn't hurt. "I was moving the hose in the front yard, when my arm bent and jerked up, my hand twisted and all the fingers curled together really tight. I couldn't bend my arm or open my hand for a while."

The incident scared me. I called our family doctor right away. Thirty minutes later, we sat in the doctor's office answering questions and listening to him make arrangements for immediate tests. The results showed eight small, scattered tumors on the left side of Red's brain. He started taking radiation treatments. Prayers began at once. I prayed in the morning, in the afternoon, in the evening. I prayed in the dark hours of night. I would sometimes hold Red's hand and ask God to dry up those tumors, to give us more time together. Family and friends began praying for healing. Missionary friends in three countries added their prayers. I knew God would answer those prayers. I believed with all my heart, mind, and soul that Red would be healed, and we would have more years together. After all, Jesus said, "Therefore I tell you, whatever you ask for in prayer, believe that you have received it, and it will be yours" (Mark 11:24).

Red gradually became more quiet and thoughtful. One time he said, "If I'm not here, I want you to take care of yourself. The house is paid for, and everything is in good condition." Another time he said, "If I'm not here, I want you to find a good husband. I don't want you living alone the rest of your life."

We were in our sixties and still had a lot of living yet to do. Whenever he talked about me being alone, I screamed on the inside, *Stop! Stop talking like that! We'll have more time. I know we will.* On the outside, I would kiss him and assure him that God would heal him, that we would share more hours and days. I tried to pass on my trust of healing to him. When his left lung collapsed and a difficult procedure had to be endured, God carried us though that trial with His grace and mercy. I was sure God would heal Red this time.

Even when radiation pneumonia attacked his body, I did not doubt his recovery. As Red lay on the emergency room gurney, we held hands. "Do you think it's okay to pray, stretched out here with my eyes closed?" he asked.

"Of course it's okay," I assured him, "You're going to be fine."

Five days later I stopped praying for healing. With my sons by my side, I made funeral arrangements for my husband. Later, in my lonely hours, I caved in to, "You betrayed me, Lord. You let my husband die. You didn't heal him. You didn't answer my prayers. Why not?"

I still believed that God answers prayers, but the only prayer I could pray was, "Why didn't You answer my prayers?" Then a brief note arrived from a beloved praying friend.

"Dear June, God *did* heal Red. God *did* answer your prayers, all our prayers. Red is whole and well now. He is with the Lord. Red will never slip into a coma, like the doctor thought he might, with the strong possibility of no recovery. Remember, God always answers our prayers. God loves you, and so do I."

I struggled to accept her words. I knew she was right, but I wanted my husband alive and well, standing right beside me. In time, however, I began to understand that when God's answer sounds like no, we need to look carefully and see if He isn't really saying yes.

Although a number of years have passed since Red went to be with our Lord, I still remember the note that came when I desperately needed assurance that God truly does answer prayers. In some hard and difficult times since Red's death, I have clung to Jesus' promise that if we pray and believe, whatever we ask for is ours. And sometimes I have to remind myself that no is an answer.

We all want to hold on to our loved ones for as long as possible. Roger and his family had a difficult time watching his mother lie in pain and suffering. They had to reach the point when they were ready to "let go." Saying good-bye is never easy, but when we trust in the Lord for His will to be done, we can usher our loved ones into new life in heaven.

The Prayer

BY ROGER ALLEN COOK, TAYLOR, MICHIGAN

I was describing my mother's desperate physical condition to my pastor after the morning service one Sunday when he solemnly asked me, "Have you prayed *The Prayer?*" I knew exactly what he meant. His compassionate question touched me deeply. Pastors seem to have a way of doing that.

Mom had been suffering from Alzheimer's disease for more than ten years, and the continuing progress of the malady was devastating. Her ability to speak had been gone for some time, and she had been forced to depend on facial expressions to communicate. Now even that was gone, as was almost any ability for independent movement, leaving her in need of total care. My dad was always the first in line to serve. He spent hours each day patiently coaxing his beloved wife to eat and take in fluids. He always told people, "She would have done this for me if the circumstances were reversed."

Having gone from a delightful woman of great mental acuity to a noncommunicative, almost comatose patient was a dramatic descent. Now she had stopped eating and rarely opened her eyes. She made a pact with Dad when she had first been diagnosed that no extreme measures would be allowed to artificially prolong life as her condition deteriorated. No feeding tubes or breathing assistance would be employed to prevent her earthly exit. Dad was committed to this agreement, but found that keeping it was a gut-wrenching experience.

That Sunday I left after speaking with my pastor and went to the nursing home to join my father at her bedside. Even in an unconscious condition, she was beginning to show grimaces of pain. I asked Dad if he was ready to give her up and pray *The Prayer*. He understood the ramifications of what I was saying. This is a man who had committed his finances, his time, and, most importantly of all, his physical health to her care. He had a real concern that he would not live long enough to see his mission through to the end. Little did he understand how close his arduous work would take him toward his own physical collapse.

He responded to my question by saying that he was ready to pray *The Prayer*. Seeing her suffering and deteriorating condition had finally moved him to let go of that which he had worked so hard to keep. On that Sunday, around noon, we prayed (my father, my wife, and I) and asked God to take the one we loved so much to heaven, if it was His will. We had no idea how God would respond to that heartfelt request, but we had prayed the prayer of release with sincerity and all due gravity. We knew that God does all things well, and this situation would be no different. We knew that what we called *The Prayer* was simply a letting go, a release of the situation totally to God.

This special prayer is simply one of asking God to take home His child who is suffering greatly. We asked God to take her home as soon as possible, but according to His will. As much as we hated to lose her, we knew that she had a great reward waiting for her. In *The Prayer* we asked God to give Mom relief from her earthly body that had so completely failed to function. This prayer is not easy to pray when you have spent so many years fighting for someone's health and then, because of the person's condition, you finally realize you must let your loved one go.

On Monday morning I went back to the nursing home to check on Mom and see Dad before teaching my class. I work at a school within walking distance of the nursing home. After a short visit I crossed the room, intending to go back over to the school, but could find no freedom in my spirit to exit. It was as if God spoke to my heart and said, "Don't leave." I removed my coat, returned to her bedside, and waited.

As the time passed, my memory painted wonderful experiences of the past on the canvas of my consciousness until I noticed that her breathing had slowed. A nurse came by to check her pulse and found it to be very faint. She told us that Mom could linger for days or even weeks in this condition. Dad knew there was a problem, he later told me, because her hand was growing colder. I sensed the difficulty of the situation and began mentally noting the widening time between her labored breaths. It was only a few minutes later that my mother stepped into eternity. She exhaled her last earthly breath and immediately inhaled her first breath of heaven.

Twenty-one hours after we said *The Prayer,* God took her home. I thank the Lord for answering so quickly and allowing me the privilege of witnessing the last moments of one of the godliest women I have ever known. The experience makes me want to shout out loud "Isn't God's grace a wonderful thing?" He gave her dying grace, when the time was right. He gave my dad comforting grace for pain that can only be felt by one committed to a lifetime of loving and caring for another.

And yes, real men do cry.

Loved ones pass on whether we are ready or not. In most cases, we rest assured in the knowledge our loved ones have entered the kingdom of heaven to be with our Lord. In some cases, we may not be too sure. The Lord is only too willing to help us discover the answer. All we need do is ask, just as Andrea did.

Heaven in My Dreams

BY ANDREA BOESHAAR, MILWAUKEE, WISCONSIN

I remember so clearly the day my dad died. It was a Saturday, late in September. The treetops were aflame with vibrant red, gold, and orange hues. It was warm and sunny, not a single cloud in the azure sky. A perfect autumn day.

Gazing out the window, I was just getting ready to climb out of bed when the phone rang. "Your father is in our emergency room." I could hear the sounds of a bustling hospital in the background, along with the nurse's carefully chosen words. "A blood vessel has burst in his abdomen, and we're taking him to surgery."

"Tell her to call Amy." My dad's voice trailed in the background behind the nurse's words.

Once our phone conversation ended, I called my sister as our dad had requested. "Amy, I just got a call from the hospital. Dad had a blood vessel burst in his abdomen, and they're taking him in for surgery immediately."

I rushed to get dressed, but since I had worked in another medical facility as an emergency-room registrar, I felt that if my dad was well enough to speak, I did not need to panic. I figured the doctors would fix whatever vessel had burst, and Dad would be fine. But I didn't waste any time. I wanted to get to the hospital as soon as possible.

Unfortunately, I found every red light along the way and even made a wrong turn as I neared the medical complex.

At long last, I found my way to the emergency room. "Andrea?" A nurse met me right away. "You look like your brother, John, so I knew it was you." The nurse showed me to my dad's room, but he had just been wheeled off to surgery. Grabbing hold of my elbow, the nurse propelled me down the hallway after the gurney.

"It's okay," I said. "I don't want to disrupt the flow of things. I just want the doctors to do their job."

"No, you don't understand, Andrea. Your father has an aortic aneurysm that ruptured. You need to see him before surgery because… well, you might not see him alive again."

I nodded in spite of my feelings of shock and thought back to my medical days. I remembered something about "Triple-A" (abdominal aortic aneurysm), and suddenly realized the severity of my dad's condition.

I jogged down the hallway beside the nurse, but my father's gurney disappeared through doors that forbid public entry. It was too late. I missed seeing my dad by mere seconds.

If only I had dressed faster or sped through those stoplights. I'm sure law-enforcement officials would have understood, considering the gravity of the situation. If only I had known!

I found my brother back in the emergency room. He did not appear frazzled in the least, and his outward calm diminished my inner tumult, convincing me that everything was going to be fine.

The medical personnel escorted John and me to a private family waiting area. Once they were gone, I questioned my brother.

"The doctor said *if* he makes it, Andrea." I listened to his uncertainty.

"What do you mean *if?*" I tried to remain optimistic. "John, I've had to register people in worse shape. This is nothing. Believe me, Dad's going to be fine."

After a few silent moments, I got curious. "What was the last thing you said to Dad?"

"I told him I loved him and then kissed him on his forehead." The poignant scene I imagined between father and son touched me deeply. "Did he hear what the doctor said—the 'if he makes it' remark?"

My brother nodded.

Collecting my emotions, I called my husband and three adult sons. I relayed everything I knew and told them to come to the hospital—just in case. My sister showed up with her two small children in tow. And we waited and prayed.

Hours passed before the surgeon finally entered the waiting room. By that time, Amy's husband and John's wife, my husband and our three sons, along with one daughter-in-law had all arrived. The doctor explained Dad's medical situation, but it didn't seem to make sense.

I looked to one of my sons, Rick, the paramedic. "He's going to die, isn't he?"

Rick nodded and slipped his arm around my shoulder, and I burst into tears as we made our way to the surgical intensive care unit.

When we arrived at Dad's room, I got the impression that he had died in the operating room. The machine hooked up to him simply kept his chest moving up and down, up and down.

My brother gave the okay to take Dad off life support. My sister and I both agreed, and the apparatus was removed. My brother and sister spoke their good-byes, but I said nothing, sensing Dad was not really there. His heart beat slower, slower, slower, and then it beat no more.

An incredible sense of loss filled the room, rivaling the afternoon sunshine spilling through the windows. I turned and walked back to the waiting area where my son Rick had stayed behind with Amy's two young children.

"Papa's gone," I told him.

I looked into Rick's face and saw complete and utter sadness streaming from my son's blue eyes. I had not seen him cry like that since he was a little boy.

During the days that followed, John, Amy, and I settled our dad's estate, and one week later his remains were buried in a lovely nearby cemetery. We all agreed that Dad would have approved of his funeral, the reception that followed, and his final resting place.

However, I was beginning to feel troubled about my dad's *real,* final resting place, the eternal one. Was Dad in heaven?

Over the last decade, my father and I had discussed spiritual matters at great length, and I always sensed he had religion, not a relationship with the Lord Jesus Christ. My husband, sons, and I had always prayed for his salvation, just as we would for anyone who was lost.

So where was Dad?

With a troubled spirit, I prayed, "God, please show me where my father is. Is he with You? Please let me know in a way I'll understand."

Now I want to be very careful in describing what happened next. I am not whacked out on any funky theology; I am just your average, Bible-believing Christian. However, one night I had the most remarkable dream. I dreamed I saw my father.

"Dad!" It seemed so real. The sight of him brought an enormous sense of joy. I asked the question weighing so heavily on my heart: "Dad, are you in heaven?"

With a white hankie in one hand, he sniffed back tears and nodded. "I just made it."

The verse in Revelation about God wiping away all tears from our eyes came to mind. I wondered why my dad was weeping. Were they tears of remorse? Regret? But I immediately let go of my questions. The most important thing to me was sensing that, at some point, my father trusted in the Lord Jesus. Dad was in heaven with the Savior!

All too soon, the dream was over. I woke up, exhausted and sobbing. The emotional toll of the past weeks poured over me, yet I knew where my dad was.

I also realized something else. I concluded that the Lord threw roadblocks on purpose into my path that Saturday morning as I made my way to the hospital. Because He did so, my father heard the doctor say there was little hope of making it through surgery. What's more, it was no accident I did not catch up to his gurney. The Lord knew I would see Dad again. He was simply giving him the small window of time to prepare his soul to meet his Maker.

One of the criminals crucified with Jesus was afforded the same opportunity. He acknowledged his personal wrongdoings, realizing he deserved his punishment and that Jesus hung beside him, completely innocent. "Then he said, 'Jesus, remember me when you come into your kingdom.' Jesus answered him, 'I tell you the truth, today you will be with me in paradise'" (Luke 23:42-43).

What a loving, compassionate God we serve. He is a God of second, third, and fourth chances. "He is patient with you, not wanting anyone to perish, but everyone to come to repentance" (2 Peter 3:9).

What's more, He is our God who answers prayers, the One who so mercifully gave me peace of mind and showed me a shining sliver of heaven in my dreams.

6
A Change of Heart

Of all the miracles of answered prayer, surely one of the most profound is that of a changed heart. Sometimes it is *our* heart that God changes, and sometimes it is the heart of the one we are praying for. In either case, it is a miracle!

The following wonderful stories demonstrate God's willingness to change hearts. If there is a person in your life who needs a change of heart, do not give up asking God to accomplish what may seem like an impossibility. Proverbs 21:1 tells us that even the heart of a king can be changed by our mighty God.

Keep praying for that loved one! *God will hear.*

> *The king's heart is in the hand of the LORD, like the rivers of water;*
> *He turns it wherever He wishes* (Proverbs 21:1 NKJV).

The pressures of being a teenager can be overwhelming. We not only have peer pressure, often there is the pressure to please our teachers and parents, too. When that pressure became too much to bear, Rusty found prayer to be his only resource and found God more than willing to answer him. All he had to do was listen.

Fireplug No More

BY RUSTY FISCHER, ORLANDO, FLORIDA

Football became a ruling force in my life when I was just a little kid. Okay, let's face it. I never really was a little kid. I was always chunky, hefty, short for my age, pudgy, stout, tubby, robust, portly. You get the picture.

Our Mighty Mights football league did not have an age limit. It had a weight requirement instead. If you were heavy enough, you got to play. I was heavy enough at eight years old. I was so big that I started playing football a whole year ahead of my friends!

The only problem was that, by the time I turned 13, I was *too* heavy. You had to weigh a certain amount to start playing, but when you weighed too much, they made you stop.

That would have been just fine with me. Five years of football practice every day after school and games all day Saturday for six months out of the year was plenty for me. I would have been happier sitting at home reading a book, if it wasn't for Dad.

Dad loved stopping by practice every day to watch me play football. Game days were like Christmas for him, hearing his son's name being called over the loudspeaker whenever I would make a big tackle or a great block. Quitting was never an option. I couldn't let my Dad down. So in I went, hating every second, day after day, week after week, year after year.

Until I was 13 and I weighed over 200 pounds. I thought that would be the end of it, once and for all. In a way, it was....

To make certain each kid was under the official weight limit every Saturday, the referees lugged one of those old-fashioned doctor's scales around with them to every game. If the scales tipped past 200, off went the unlucky player's cleats, then the helmet, the shoulder pads, the jersey, the pants, or even the undershirt and socks. Coach knew I was heading for trouble the day I had to step out of my underwear just to make weight.

The very next Monday at practice he presented me with an attractive T-shirt made out of a black garbage bag.

"Put it on," he grunted, pointing out the ragged holes for my head and arms. "Start running around the practice field, and don't stop until I say so."

I would wave at him questioningly after every single lap, while my friends got to sit on their helmets and talk about the latest *Mad* magazine or *Star Wars* movie—in between laughing and pointing at me, that is.

"Keep going, Fireplug," Coach would grunt around the mushy cigar in his mouth.

That was my nickname: Fireplug. Although no one ever explained it to me, I figured it had something to do with me being shaped like a fire hydrant.

Every day at practice I had to run laps in that stupid garbage bag. I would hear it crinkling beneath my underarms as I stumbled through the stickers and the weeds, lap after lap. My short, stocky legs weren't exactly graceful, and I would often fall or stumble. The other players would laugh, but not as loud as Coach. The only one who didn't laugh at me was my dad. Although I know it must have embarrassed him to see his chubby son running around the field wearing a garbage-bag T-shirt, he still showed up every day at practice to cheer me on.

When the garbage-bag T-shirt did not exactly work wonders, Coach arranged for me to use the sauna at one of the local high-rise condominiums that dotted the beach town I grew up in.

The very next Saturday, Coach handed me my garbage-bag T-shirt and wedged me into a cedar-lined closet with two benches and a red metal shelf full of glowing, hot rocks. He poured water on the rocks to build up the steam and shut the door on me with a wicked smile.

Outside the little porthole window, I could see him chomping on glazed donuts and sipping a cup of coffee.

My stomach roared. Since it was a game day, I hadn't eaten since dinner the night before. Nor would I be eating again until after the weigh-in. I sat there dripping sweat and realized something was very wrong with this picture. It was Saturday morning. There I was, sitting in a sweatbox, while the rest of the team chomped on Frosted Flakes and watched cartoons. They were still in their pajamas, while I was here in a garbage-bag sweat suit. Why?

Was I being punished for something? Were the running and the sweating and the hunger and the pain not enough? What more did they want?

The only thing left to do in that boiling sauna was to pray. I could barely sit up, let alone get down on bended knee, but I prayed nonetheless.

"Dear God," I whispered, spraying sweat from my upper lip and watching it turn to vapor before my very eyes, "guide me. Please tell me if I'm being just a wimp, or if this is really one of those moments. Is this one of those life-changing moments that forever alter your future, where you make a stand and come out better for it on the other end? Please help me to understand what You want me to do. Amen."

In the silence following my heartfelt prayer, I suddenly realized I had been knocking myself out for something I didn't want to do in the first place and didn't have to do anymore. My heart fluttered and my stomach flip-flopped, but I stood up on wobbly legs and walked out of the sauna. It didn't exactly seem brave, it just seemed... right.

"Did I say you could get out of there?" Coach bellowed.

"I quit," I said in a shaky voice.

"You *quit?*" he fairly laughed, looming over me in his ever-present coaching shorts. "You can't quit. What would your dad think? Don't you want him to be proud of you anymore?"

But that was just it. If Dad couldn't be proud of me for just being me, then what was the point? Coach called my dad. But it didn't matter to me anymore. I had finally made up my mind. It was time to be proud of myself for a change, no matter what anyone else thought.

When Coach had explained the situation to my dad, he grunted and handed over the phone. I was glad I was not doing this face-to-face. My hands were shaking so badly I could hardly hold the phone. Suddenly my bravery in the sauna vanished in the steam-filled pool room. What if he really freaked out and disowned me? Would I have to go live with Coach?

"Son," my dad said quietly, "is what Coach said true?"

"Yes," I whispered into the phone.

"You don't want to play football anymore?" he asked simply.

Well, if I was going to do this, I was going to do it right. "I never did," I gasped.

Dad's laughter surprised me. "Then why did you go through with all of those shenanigans?" he asked. "I thought you wanted to be the next Joe Namath!"

I hung up the phone and headed for my bike. Coach stood there fuming as I pedaled away. Although I quit football for good that year, I did have Coach to thank for one thing: I took up jogging—something that I have stuck with ever since.

I learned to love and respect the simple joy of feeling my own sweat on my skin, the breeze in my face, and the in and out of my breathing as I loped leisurely about my small beach town. Without a sweat-soaked garbage bag wrinkling in my ear, I was able to hear the ocean around me and enjoy the solitude of the simple morning run.

With the help of the Lord, I started carrying myself differently and respecting myself more. I grew a little, shaped up, learned a lot, and eventually the name Fireplug just seemed to fade with time.

Except for one night. My family and I were waiting for a table in a local restaurant lobby when Coach sauntered in on his way to the bar.

He greeted my dad rather coolly, and then eyed me with open disdain. "What's the word, Fireplug?" he asked.

Dad looked at me for an instant, and then corrected Coach firmly. "You meant Rusty, right, Coach?"

Coach grumbled something through the mushy cigar in his mouth, but it didn't matter. Our table was ready, and Dad kept his hand on my shoulder the entire way there.

And no one ever called me Fireplug again.

What can be more painful for a parent than to see a child make the wrong choices? Many, many parents have labored long and hard in prayer over a son or daughter who has taken the wrong road. In the case of Bob and Fran Haslam, that wrong road led their daughter into spiritual deception. But God hears the prayers of concerned parents. We must never stop praying for our children, no matter how old they are or how safe their path may *seem* to be. A parent's intercession for a child must never cease.

A Day of Miracles

BY BOB HASLAM, LYNNWOOD, WASHINGTON

Little did my wife and I know what we faced when we moved from Indiana to the Chicago area. I had accepted a position with a Christian relief organization, while my wife found temporary employment in a teaching position. What began in January mushroomed into serious problems by that summer.

We left our empty home in Indiana in the hands of what turned out to be an incompetent real estate agent. Months passed and there was no movement on selling our property. We had a bridging loan to buy the townhouse we had moved into, and at the time the principal on the loan was almost 20 percent. We were strapped.

At the end of the school year, my wife's temporary teaching position ended, as did her paycheck. She began looking for an opening throughout the area school systems, without finding a readily available job. Day after day she made appointments for interviews, only to be disappointed.

But financial woes pale in comparison to what came next.

We discovered that our 20-year-old daughter had become caught up in a dangerous cult in California. My wife begged me to go there and force our daughter to come home. Friends at work told me that if it was their daughter, they would be on the next plane to California without any second thought.

Yet for some reason, I felt restrained. As I prayed for my daughter, I never felt the Lord's release to make the trip and try to extricate our daughter from the clutches of the cult. God's leading was confirmed when I phoned the police near the town where my daughter was living and was told that because of her age I would be charged with kidnapping if I were to forcefully take her from California.

Day after day I went to work, praying constantly for our daughter's deliverance. Daily my wife continued looking for a job. Having her work was necessary to our financial stability. But in the evening and on into the night, we agonized over our daughter's situation.

Every night before going to bed, my wife and I read the Scriptures and prayed. We firmly placed our daughter in God's hands and asked for her rescue. Then when we got under the covers, I went to sleep, but my wife remained awake for hours.

One night I was divinely led to read a passage in the ninth chapter of the Gospel of Mark. The story is told of a man who brought his son to Jesus—a boy who was controlled by an evil spirit. The father said to Jesus, "From childhood…it [the spirit] has often thrown him into fire or water to kill him. But if you can do anything, take pity on us and help us."

"If you can?" said Jesus. "Everything is possible for him who believes."

The father's reply has become a classic statement: "I do believe; help me overcome my unbelief!" In response to his faltering faith, Jesus healed the young lad.

My attention focused on the initial words of the father who pleaded for his son: "But if you can do anything, take pity on us and help us." *If You can!*

I pointed out those words to my wife. "That's how we've been praying," I conceded. "We've been praying to God, and at the same time wondering if He can do anything in our situation."

My wife was swift with her response. "Write 'We believe!' in the margin of the Bible."

I did so and also wrote the date.

Days passed, running into weeks. But now we prayed differently than before, believing God *could* and *would* answer our prayers.

Now we had three major requests before the Lord: One, for our daughter's deliverance. Two, a teaching job for my wife. And three, the sale of our empty home back in Indiana.

On a hot and muggy summer afternoon, I sat at my desk at work when the phone rang. It was our new realtor back in Indiana. "I have a firm offer on your home," she said. "I'll fax you the paperwork; you and your wife sign it and fax it back."

I drove home with the exciting news. When I opened the door to the house, I hurried to the kitchen and said to my wife, "Guess what?"

"Guess what yourself!" she replied. "I just received a call from a school superintendent offering me a job."

"Wow!" I responded. "And our house sold today. Can you believe that?"

My wife looked at me with misty eyes and said, "You know, all we need to have happen to make this a perfect day is for our daughter to call and ask to come home."

That sobered us both.

Supper over, I went out to the car to go to the mall on an errand. As I turned into the street, out of the corner of my eye I saw motion. My wife was frantically waving her arms and calling. I stopped the car and rolled down the window.

"Grace is on the phone and wants to talk to you," she shouted.

Grace! Our daughter!

I left the car at the curb and ran across the street, the yard, and into the house. "Hello?"

The first words I heard were, "Dad, can I come home?"

"Yes!" I shouted. "Yes! We *want* you to come home."

This was one month to the day after we wrote in our Bible, "We believe!"

Our daughter was calling from an airport.

"Stay right where you are," I told her. "Call back in one hour. I'm on my way to the mall, and I'll go to the travel agency and buy a ticket for you."

That same night she flew the "red-eye" flight from the West Coast to Chicago. On Saturday morning, we met her as she came off the plane. She rushed into our arms as we embraced her with tears.

The next day at church I shared with our praying friends our amazing day with three major answers to prayer—three miracles at once. I wept as I told them the awesome story.

One of our friends came up to me and said, "All the while you were crying, God was smiling, knowing how perfectly He was about to orchestrate your life!"

Yes, our God delights in answering prayer. Never before had we seen His mighty power at work in such a spectacular display of grace and mercy. Today we rest in that peace that passes all understanding. When we believe, God opens the doors of heaven, pouring out His blessings and miracles as He answers the deepest prayers of our heart.

What if I get in an accident on the way home from work? What if my husband has a heart attack and dies? What if my child develops a fatal disease? What if…What if…What if…Worry robs us of living a life filled with joy and thanksgiving. Ann triumphed over worry when she called out to God in prayer.

POW

BY ANNE JOHNSON, KEARNEY, NEBRASKA

Why isn't she mad at God? I wondered. I stared at my friend Barb and her family as they grieved at the hospital over the death of her baby. I questioned God's love. My face reddened. *God, You are so unfair.*

Barb's demonstration of faith during this horrific time astounded me. She did not ask why her baby died, nor did she curse God; instead, she *prayed*. She asked God to use this situation to draw other people closer to Him.

Shame swirled about me like a tornado as I thanked God for not letting this happen to me. Six months prior, God had blessed my husband and me with a healthy baby girl. Now I could not help but wonder, *What if we had lost our baby?* I knew I would never be as strong as Barb. I knew prayer would be the last thing I would think to do.

I hugged the mourning family and fled to the one place in the hospital where I hoped to find peace. I hesitantly walked toward the front of the chapel.

Welcomed by the flickering light of a solitary candle and serene silence, I fought to control my racing heart and mind. "Barb is such a wonderful mother. Why would You do this, God?" I whimpered. "Lord, if You did this to such a godly woman, what will You do to me? What will You do to my newborn child? Please, God, don't take my baby away."

I knelt on the chapel floor, a vision of Barb filling my mind. She held her husband's hand as she prayed. The pressure in my chest increased as I recalled her courageous words: "I trust You, Lord. You alone are in control. Use this to draw others closer to You."

I yielded my tired body to the quiet darkness in the chapel as I drifted into a fitful slumber…and I dreamed.

The abusers rip me from my cold cell and drag my broken body down the dark, malodorous hall. My broken legs refuse to support me. The captor's bony fingers dig into my arms as they pull me down the hallway past the wailing and moaning of the other prisoners.

With every breath, pain surges through my aching body. I gasp for air as hideous demons throw me before their king. His hot, fiery breath stings my tear-filled eyes.

"You stupid, no-good, worthless creature," the fiends hiss, striking me. The wounds are deep and the pain intense.

I am a POW, a prisoner of war in Satan's grasp.

"Where are You, God?" I call.

Through the ominous blackness enveloping my mind, I hear the sounds of people passionately praying. I struggle to open my eyes, to return to the present.

The chill was gone. I awoke in the dimly lighted chapel.

"Thank God, it was only a dream," I gasped. Then reality hit me like one of my captor's fists; I was still in the hospital chapel. The urgent supplications were coming from a family praying for their loved one.

I struggled to get my aching knees to straighten. Tears filled my eyes as I recalled the reason for my presence here. Just 12 hours after delivery, God called Barb's precious infant home. Pain flooded my heart; intense pressure wrenched the air from my lungs. How will she ever go on? I know I couldn't!

What if God calls my baby girl home? I am not a perfect mother, and in my daughter's first six months, I have made many mistakes. Tormented by these thoughts, I begged God to have mercy on me.

Like in my dream, I am a prisoner to fear and worries. My head pounded like a blacksmith hammering a piece of metal on his anvil.

I closed my eyes and fell back onto the altar. "Help me, God," I prayed.

Silence. Maybe God doesn't care. Maybe I am alone. My breathing is rapid.

"*POW*" came a soft whisper.

Though the room was silent, I strained to hear the quiet voice.

"My precious child, don't you know your enemy wants to keep you imprisoned by fear and worry? Satan wants the difficult circumstances in your life to cripple you and steal your joy. But you don't have to be a POW in Satan's clutches. Instead fix your eyes on Me, and I will lift you above every situation."

"Oh Father," my heart cried out, "forgive me for doubting You. Help me to treasure every day with my baby. Help me to be the mother You created me to be. Please help Barb and her family get through this situation. And please show me how to overcome these crippling thoughts."

"POW," He repeated.

"I don't understand," I said.

"If you will look to Me, I will give you Power Over Worry (POW)."

I bowed my head and confessed my feelings of inadequacy. I admitted my doubts about His perfect plan for my life, as well as for the life of my infant. I sought forgiveness for not considering the power of prayer in my everyday life.

Though silence continued to abide in the room, God's warm, peaceful presence rushed toward me and lifted my fears.

I felt empowered as I headed back toward the postpartum unit. Though this painful situation had not vanished, I no longer felt entrapped by the fear of losing my own child.

Rather than listening to the lies of my enemy or continuing to be Satan's POW, I found strength in knowing that when I pray, God will bear my burdens, giving me the ultimate Power Over Worry.

In a world full of instant food, instant communication, and instant gratification, it's so easy to ask God why He has not answered our prayer "right now." The struggle of good versus evil can be a constant war. With Satan around every corner, watching every move, we cannot afford to stop our prayers for a minute. Pastors Lowell and Connie Lundstrom never stopped praying for their lost sheep, and in God's time she returned home to the fold. God won and victory was theirs.

My Precious Prodigal

BY LOWELL LUNDSTROM, SAVAGE, MINNESOTA

"Reverend Lundstrom?"

"This is Reverend Lundstrom. May I help you?"

"I need you to meet me at the police station, sir. Your 17-year-old daughter is scheduled to appear in court for propositioning a vice-officer."

My hands trembled as I hung up the receiver. I was numb as I wove my way through traffic toward the main precinct.

My daughter—a prostitute? Impossible!

My wife and I had dedicated Lisa to the Lord as a baby. We raised her on Bible stories, gospel songs, and prayer. *There must be some mistake.*

The reality of this nightmare was like getting hit in the chest with a cement block. The vice-officer opened the police file, read his account of her proposition, and showed me her mug shot. My knees buckled, and I almost fainted. There was no mistake. My precious daughter was a hooker, working the streets in a major midwestern city.

I knew Lisa had been going through a spiritual struggle for a long time, and I tried to warn her about the dangers of living in a spiritually cold condition. But I never dreamed in my worst nightmares that my daughter would become a prostitute.

When the Lord won my heart in April 1957, my wife and I began singing, preaching, and evangelizing immediately. We started a radio ministry called *Message for America*. And we conducted citywide evangelistic events, where hundreds of thousands of people came to Christ.

Lisa was the second child of four, and Londa, her older sister, was very talented musically. Lisa was, too; however, she did not really enjoy singing to a crowd like Londa did. One of her brothers, Lowell Jr., was also a hit with the crowds. Lance, our youngest, was a quiet boy, and Lisa took him under her wing, taking care of him when he was a baby.

Somehow, in the midst of all the ministry activities, I failed to see that Lisa was hurting. She was more academically inclined, and audiences seemed to applaud Londa and Lowell's music more than hers.

Failing to see Lisa's hurt and the unresolved conflict in her soul, I had no idea a root of bitterness was building in her spirit. She never gave us any problems, but her own inner anxieties were ticking away like a time bomb.

I continued touring and evangelizing, reaching other people for Christ, but failing to see my own precious daughter silently fading away from God and our family.

After she appeared in court, the judge committed Lisa to my care. I was given jurisdiction over her activities, but the situation was so volatile that Lisa was almost immediately placed in a halfway house for teen prostitutes.

Lisa soon escaped and headed south, under the influence of what the judge described as the worst pimp in the region. "I've been trying to get this man behind bars for many years," the judge had told me.

"He's too slick. He avoids getting caught, or wins in court with the help of his clever attorneys."

I was devastated. My daughter had chosen a pimp as her mentor, rejecting me as her father.

I knew that raising my children in the high tension of frontline crusade evangelism created pressure for my family, and there was always risk, but I had made a deal with God when I surrendered to His ministry. "Lord, I'll give You my whole life to help Your lost children, but You must stand guard over my family. Protect them from Satan."

But Lisa was gone. And worst of all, I felt God had double-crossed me.

Sometimes we would not hear from Lisa for months at a time, and during those periods of silence, we did not know if she was dead or alive. I felt that God had betrayed me.

But despite all of this, I kept traveling and preaching 300 nights a year. As much as I felt that God had let me down, I still loved Him, believed in Him, and preached His message as faithfully as I could. Multitudes were coming to Christ—except the one I wanted to call home.

Knowing that pimps or crazed clients often kill prostitutes, I purchased newspapers from every major city and searched obituary columns for news about unidentified bodies found by railroad tracks or near rivers.

Lisa was truly lost. I knew that Jesus Christ, the great Shepherd, was the only One who could find my precious daughter. I cast myself on His mercy, asking for prayer during every evangelical meeting. "Please pray for my Lisa." Without explaining the details, I alerted believers that she needed God's help.

Finally I reached the point where I did not care what other people thought. All I knew was that I wanted my precious prodigal back.

One day I visited another minister. His son had gotten involved in drugs and committed suicide. He never said much about this to other people, but he told me privately, "Lowell, I believe God has his soul, but the devil got his body."

His words prompted me to summon intercessors to help me pray. Over the next several years, I asked nearly every group I ministered to, to join me in praying for Lisa.

I replayed scenes from Lisa's childhood in my mind over and over. I tormented myself by reviewing my failure to see her hurts and needs. In some ways, I was a prodigal parent. I found myself repeating phrases like, "I should have," "I could have," "I would have," and "If only."

Struggling with self-condemnation, I watched some of my ministry staff quit. They felt I was no longer a man they could look up to. In fact, a few told me that I should quit preaching and get out of the ministry, implying that because my daughter was living a sinful lifestyle, I was unfit to stand in the pulpit.

Maybe they're right. Maybe I should quit the ministry. Maybe I am unfit to be an evangelist.

One dark night, when I had all but given up, the Holy Spirit spoke to my heart: "Lowell, what did God do wrong, that the devil went bad?"

Suddenly hope shined through the darkness. God revealed to me that even though I had made mistakes as a father, I was not totally responsible for Lisa's actions. I had not abandoned her, and this revealing moment helped steady me.

I determined to reach every prodigal young person I came into contact with, trusting God to reach my unreachable daughter. I began to view every troubled teenage girl as if she was someone else's "Lisa." I did the same for the rebellious young men.

I was certain the Lord would save Lisa within months, but the years continued rolling by. In fact, eight long years rolled by. The enemy impressed upon me that it was futile to pray any longer. Lisa was lost—completely lost. And after years of intercession, I came to the point where I prayed, "God, if You can't save Lisa, I don't want to go to heaven either." I had reached my breaking point.

When Lisa first went astray, I would send her long letters assuring her of my love. I also included Scriptures, hoping the truth of God's Word would enlighten her, but these letters only distanced her from me.

My wife and I gradually became aware that we still had a tenuous link to Lisa, so we started building emotional bridges using every special event in the calendar year to send cards and gifts. This began to soften the barrier.

We wanted to have our daughter home. Finally, after nine years, Lisa decided to come home for Christmas. Connie and I worked hard to decorate the tree and our home, preparing for Lisa's visit. Our time as a family that Christmas was filled with reminiscing and laughter, but when Lisa decided to go back to her "lifestyle," we knew that we were losing her again.

One night Lisa made a call on a "customer." She soon discovered that he was a serial killer who had murdered 18 women, and she was destined to be number 19. He put a knife to her throat and stretched her out on a plastic garbage bag. For several hours, he ran knives up and down her body, preparing to kill her. Lisa silently called out, "Please, God, don't let me die like this. I don't want my family to learn it ended this way!" The presence of God filled the room, and she felt the Holy Spirit push back the black demon of death radiating from this crazed killer. Then, in an amazing turn of events, God stepped in. The serial killer set Lisa free and committed suicide.

One day while on tour in Canada, I received the happiest phone call of my life. It was Lisa, and she wanted to come home. I dropped everything, rented a moving van and a car trailer, and headed south on a 2000-mile journey—nonstop.

Forty hours later, Lisa was in my arms. We loaded her belongings and headed home. The terrible nine-and-a-half-year nightmare was over. My precious prodigal was back.

God had not failed.

Satan lost.

Jesus was faithful.

And Lisa was saved!

Five years have gone by since Lisa's return, and she is now my cohost on the "Lowell—LIVE!" radio program. She shares her story at our crusades and, as a result, more than 2000 young people have given their hearts to the Lord. She has appeared on *The 700 Club* and other television shows. She ministers at youth conventions, women's abuse centers, homeless shelters, and narcotic- and substance-abuse groups. She is also writing her autobiography.

God is faithful, and I can assure you from going through all of this that He will not fail you. At this very moment, He is working behind the scenes.

Our Father in heaven is forever faithful. Yogi Berra, the Yankee baseball catcher, said it best: "It ain't over till it's over!"

> *For our struggle is not against flesh and blood, but against the rulers, against the authorities, against the powers of this dark world and against the spiritual forces of evil in the heavenly realms. Therefore put on the full armor of God, so that when the day of evil comes, you may be able to stand your ground, and after you have done everything, to stand* (Ephesians 6:12-13).

Never, never give up! Give in—to God.

Many of us know the difficulties faced with moving an entire household and family to a new home. What if we had to do that seven times in 20 years? When Barb thought the moves were finally over, Greg told her Texas was next, and her first response was anything but loving. But when Barb turned to the Lord in prayer, she was filled with peace. Asking God to help us with a major decision in our lives can only prove to be the right course of action.

A New Heart

BY BARBARA E. HALEY, UNIVERSAL CITY, TEXAS

"What do you mean you want to move again?" I asked, anger punctuating my words. "We agreed. I will follow you 20 years, and then we will stay put!"

Though exhilarating and educational, my husband's career in the United States Air Force had also proved exhausting for our family. During his tour, we had lived in seven different locations, including an overseas assignment.

Now Greg was eligible for retirement. We had two children in college nearby, and another working in the area. I treasured my teaching position and relied on my church family for support as I dealt with a chronic physical problem. I liked where I was living, and I wanted to stay there *forever*.

But now Greg was telling me he wanted us to move from Illinois to Texas—900 miles.

Had he forgotten? We had agreed the day he enlisted: 20 years and no more.

Struggling with the anger in my heart, I prayed. "Please help me, Lord. I don't want to be this angry, but I don't know how to change."

The next day, as I walked down the hall at school, a student approached me about a problem he was having. I gave him a hug, and with a little encouragement and advice, his smile returned and he walked off, determined to overcome the challenge he faced.

I love teaching so much! I continued down the hall, giving and receiving hugs, patting backs, and whispering hellos as other students passed by.

Greg loves the Air Force that much.

Where did that come from?

You can get another teaching job wherever you move, but Greg will have to give up the Air Force if he agrees to stay here.

Okay, now I knew. I was being horribly selfish, and it was wrong. Thank You, Holy Spirit.

My heart, filled with bitterness and anger just moments before, now oozed with love and affection for my husband, as well as an overwhelming desire to help him keep the job he loved so much. God had answered my prayer by opening my eyes and softening my heart. It was truly a miracle!

Greg had flown to San Antonio for several days of meetings about the new assignment, calling me each evening. I had been rather short with him during those calls, but that evening I waited anxiously for his call, ready to apologize for my attitude and to offer him my support for his new position. But when he called, I immediately sensed a broken spirit.

"What's the matter, honey?" I asked.

"I talked to my future commanding officer today."

Pain clawed at my heart. I still dreaded the idea of moving and saying good-bye to so many people I loved and needed. But my desire for Greg's happiness now overrode my sorrow. How had I been so blind?

"I told him that I don't want to move—that I want out of the assignment."

"You did *what?*"

"Honey," he said, "I'm sorry for asking you to give up everything and move. I had no right to do that. We made a promise. I am hurting our entire family."

"Greg…"

"No. Let me finish. When I told the commander I wanted out of the assignment, he said he didn't think I realized what such a decision would do to my career. Then he told me to go think about it."

"When you come back tomorrow," the commander said, "we'll pretend this conversation never took place."

"Did you leave it at that?"

"Yes, but only after I told him I would *not* change my mind. My family is more important than my career."

The phone lines were silent, save for sobs on both ends. Finally I answered.

"God got through to me today, Greg. I'm okay with moving."

"What?" he said softly. "You've got to be kidding. Are you serious?"

I explained what had happened. "I offered my bitterness to God, and He replaced it with a desire to help you stay in the Air Force."

"Are you sure?"

"I've never been more sure of anything in my life."

We prayed together on the phone and agreed that moving was God's will, regardless of the difficult changes bound to come. And just like my precious little student, with a bit of encouragement and advice, my smile returned and I walked on, determined to overcome the challenge I faced.

God's Word is true. He promised, "I will give you a new heart and put a new spirit in you; I will remove from you your heart of stone and give you a heart of flesh" (Ezekiel 36:26).

And He did.

Marriage is a true "working" relationship. It requires time and effort and lots of prayer to keep it heading in the right direction. Thelma and George got lost on the highway. It took the intercessory prayers of friends to help show them the way home.

A Marriage Made in Heaven

BY THELMA WELLS, DALLAS, TEXAS

I truly believe many marriages which have ended in divorce were marriages made in heaven. Satan, the enemy of God and God's children, is a liar, schemer, and deceiver, and he takes pleasure in destroying what God has joined together.

If you know without a doubt that God put you and your spouse together, I encourage you to be diligent in prayer. We need to persevere when we ask Him for help and healing. Jesus said to the disciples, "I tell you the truth, if you have faith as small as a mustard seed, you can say to this mountain, 'Move from here to there' and it will move. Nothing will be impossible for you" (Matthew 17:20).

My marriage has gone through tremendous trials and temptations. At the age of 20, I entered marriage with the fairy-tale idea "…and they lived happily ever after." I soon found myself angry, frustrated, and troubled. My husband did not like to shop; left his shoes, socks, and underwear wherever they fell, expecting me to pick them up; and made major financial decisions without my input. I thought more than once, "This marriage stuff ain't all it's cracked up to be! What happened to the living happily ever after?"

More than 25 years ago I seriously considered getting a divorce. George admitted to infidelity, and that seemed to be the last straw. But thanks be to God, the Lord sent us help! I will never forget the early-morning phone call we received one Saturday in 1974. On the other end of the line was C. L. Walker.

"Are you up, Thelma?" Mr. Walker asked me.

"No, sir," I answered.

"Well, wake up and put George on the phone."

I obeyed.

"George and Thelma," Mr. Walker said, "I don't know what's going on in your house, but the Lord didn't let me sleep all night, praying for and thinking about y'all. Whatever's happening, it's not good. God is not pleased, and the two of you had better get it straight. My wife and I want to pray for you right now."

Mr. Walker and his wife then prayed words of admonition to us and petitioned God for our unity, decisions, peace, and problem solving. I could not believe somebody was praying for us! The Walkers knew nothing about our problems; we had confided in no one at the time. There was no doubt in our minds that the Holy Spirit prompted the Walkers to call us.

After praying, my husband and I went back to bed, but neither of us could go back to sleep. We lay completely silent except for the intense breathing and intermittent sobbing I was doing.

Suddenly my husband turned to me and said, "Thelma, Mr. Walker is right. I've done everything to you I guess I could have, but you've always stayed a good wife. If you forgive me for what I've done and how I've hurt you, I promise I will never deliberately do anything to hurt you again. It's over with her. I'm done with this. There's nothing out there I want more than you, and I'm not leaving you for anybody. I love you."

"I love you, too," I told him. "I hope you're being straight with me. I'll forgive you, but it'll take some time to forget. I want a whole husband, not a piece of a husband. If you can promise you will be that, I'll accept your apology."

Praise God, I can honestly say that from that time on, my husband has kept his word. He has been a whole husband. He has supported me in all my endeavors. He is my prayer partner and my greatest fan. We have gone through trials related to our finances, children, health, and more since that time, but God made our marriage in heaven. He was faithful to keep His promise to us to bless our marriage in spite of ourselves.

That fateful day renewed our relationship with each other and solidified the marriage God had divinely orchestrated for us. Satan was playing his ugly hand in our marital affairs by creating battles of discord, unfaithfulness, bitterness, and anger. But God won all the skirmishes and ultimately won the war.

At the core of everything is the amazing power of prayer. It is our conduit to God! The prayers of our Christian friends saved our marriage. Now we do not look back at what was. We appreciate what is, and look forward to wonderful tomorrows.

7
Finding Love

When God first created man, He realized that it was not good for him to be alone. Thus the creation of humanity included two genders: male and female. Down through history, God has paired up men and women. Adam and Eve, Abraham and Sarah, Isaac and Rebekah, Jacob and Rachel, and Joseph and Mary are just a few of the couples joined together by God. And what about Boaz and Ruth, brought together for a great purpose after Ruth's tragic loss of her first husband? Even the story of Hosea and Gomer reveals how God's plan can still be seen, even with a spouse who has been unfaithful.

Has God answered your prayers regarding your love life?

Read the following stories that demonstrate a wide range of answered prayers regarding love. And then continue to pray for your loved one, or for the soon arrival of the person God has created for you.

> *For this reason a man shall leave his father and his mother, and be joined to his wife; and they shall become one flesh* (Genesis 2:24 NASB).

Even though losing a loved one through divorce can be devastating, God has a plan for us. *"And we know that in all things
God works for the good of those who love him, who have been
called according to his purpose"* (Romans 8:28). Because he chose
to pray, Dennis was to find this out firsthand, even though it
seemed as if his whole life had fallen apart.

All Things for the Good

BY DENNIS VAN SCOY SR., RED OAK, IOWA

After 21 years it was over. My wife had deserted me and left me
with three teenagers to take care of. I had convinced myself our marriage was sound and that the more than two-decades-long relationship, which had started in high school, was lifelong.

It was hard to believe at the age of 38 that I was now a single
parent. I found myself in the deepest pit of despair I could ever have
imagined—heartbroken, betrayed, and even suicidal.

I guess I had grown complacent in marriage, so much so that I
missed the red flags that seem so obvious now. During our marriage,
I kept drifting farther and farther from God. I had invited Jesus into
my heart some ten years earlier, but never gave Him any Lordship
in my life, nor did anything to deepen my relationship with Him.
My wife had no real belief in God and would become furious at my
slightest interest in the Bible.

Perhaps it is in times like this that the line is drawn in the sand
regarding spiritual direction. Faced with a choice of becoming hateful
toward God for my plight and turning away from Him, or drawing
near to Him as a hurting child seeking consolation from his father,
by God's grace and mercy I chose the latter.

Now, at last, in my brokenness and despair, I came to realize how much I needed His comfort and guidance. Though my prayers were selfish at first, products of my own desperation and need, they *were* prayers. Finally I was talking to God again.

Begging Him to bring my wife back and restore my marriage, I cried out, "Lord, help me live again and make me whole. *Please.*"

Then, as days turned into weeks and weeks into months, I understood my wife had chosen a new life with someone else, staunchly refusing to return home or to agree to any type of counseling. She told me she loved this other man and that our marriage was over. Her leaving was permanent, and she would not be returning. As divorce proceedings began, I knew it was time to start committing my future to God's direction.

As I drew closer to Him through daily reading of His Word, I no longer saw Him as just a critical observer of my life, but rather as a participant with me—One who loved me and was directing me away from sin and into His will. The loneliness was still very real, however, and my heart cried out in fervent prayer for God to bring a mate into my life—one I could trust with my love and who would share in my life. The difference this time was that I was leaving the choosing to God.

"If it's Your will, God, please open doors and make it clear if You are directing me to someone. Not mine, but Your will be done." That was my heartfelt prayer.

As the leaves began to fall, I returned to work from my extended leave of absence. Relocating my family to a smaller home closer to my job, I slowly began to move forward in my life.

One day in late October, my eldest son (then 20) brought me a clipping from our local newspaper. It was an advertisement from the Parents Without Partners organization. They were having an informal gathering at the local library for anyone interested in starting up a group in our town. My children urged me to go, although I strongly resisted the idea.

Later that same evening, I parked my police cruiser across the street from the library to observe the people entering for the meeting. "Lord, please lead me in the direction You wish me to go. If it is Your will that I attend, please give me a nudge in the right direction." It had become my habit to pray for just about everything in my life, and this was no exception.

I really did not want to conspicuously enter this gathering in uniform, being an introvert at heart. I was uncomfortable with crowds, and frankly I was doubtful that attending this meeting would serve any tangible purpose in my situation.

Observing those going into the building, for the most part they seemed lackadaisical and uncertain. Some people walked toward the building as if they were resisting an unseen force pushing them to enter. Others just appeared awkward, unprepared, and apprehensive.

It was nearly time for the meeting to begin, and I was almost ready to drive away when "she" arrived. Blonde, attractive, and in her mid-thirties, she walked with poise and determination. Carrying writing supplies, she smiled at other people entering for the meeting and showed no sign of hesitation or discomfort about being in attendance.

She was indeed different. Seeing her arrive was just the nudge I needed from the Holy Spirit. I grabbed the microphone and radioed the dispatcher that I would be taking my supper break at the library.

During the meeting, I learned her name was Debbie. She radiated a sense of purpose and organization that must have been visible to all the other people as well, for they seemed to gravitate toward her. She was friendly, sensible, and intelligent, and without a single objection, the others elected her to the office of president of this newly formed organization.

Perhaps it was the uniform or just a desire by the group to equally balance the chain of command, but before I knew what was happening,

I had somehow been elected to the position of vice president of the new organization. I would be working closely with Debbie at meetings and planning sessions. It was a prospect that brought a smile to my heart.

As we began seeing each other for club business, we discovered we both shared a love for the Lord and had both placed our lives in His hands. She had divorced her first husband some six years earlier because of his continuous adulterous behavior, and was raising four young girls on her own. In fact, it was her eldest daughter who had brought her the same newspaper advertisement about the meeting at the library, and who pressured her into attending.

Debbie was exactly the opposite of my ex-wife. She was intense in her conviction regarding fidelity in relationships. She deeply believed in prayer and the teachings of the Bible. She brought me through many moments of my postdesertion depression by challenging me and encouraging me to be the man God was calling me to be. She taught me not to depend on any other human being to bring joy in my life, but to seek God first and know the joy only He could provide.

Over the next few months, we found ourselves often being brought together in many an unusual happenstance. Chance meetings, long telephone conversations, and discovery of like interests became increasingly commonplace. The more I spoke to her, the more I knew she was the kind of woman God wanted me to seek for a lasting relationship. I sensed His mighty hand opening doors, bringing us together to grow both emotionally and spiritually. I fell in love with Debbie for the godly woman she was.

The following summer Debbie and I married. That was 19 years ago now, and I am so thankful to God for His faithfulness to His Word. "And we know that in all things God works for the good of those who love him, who have been called according to his purpose"

(Romans 8:28), even out of the heartbreak of our individual pasts. God answered my lonely prayer beyond my fondest hopes.

Today we continue to honor God in our marriage and our home. Debbie has founded a vibrant women's ministry, and I know her love for me is second only to that for her wonderful Savior: Christ the Lord.

The long and winding road the Fawcett family traveled during Sharon's bitter season of depression could have ruined their family. Yet they endured a journey that few could ever imagine. The sicker Sharon got, the more Tim came to depend on God. With unceasing, unconditional love, Tim prayed his wife and their marriage back to health. Today they stand as shining examples that through God—and prayer—nothing is impossible.

A Mission of Love

BY SHARON L. FAWCETT, PETITCODIAC,
NEW BRUNSWICK, CANADA

It was one of those cold, gray spring mornings that make a soul wonder if the earth will ever bloom again. My heart was heavy and as lifeless as the day itself. The grass was brown and soggy underfoot as I walked across the yard to the house. *I wonder how long I'll be gone?* I thought, as I entered through the side door.

My little girls were inside, waiting for "Mommy." One-year-old Jenna tottered into the entryway when she saw me, still quite unstable with her new skill of walking. Four-year-old Lauren followed closely behind her sister, eyes wide, looking like a concerned little mother with arms ready to catch Jenna should she stumble.

As I watched them make their way toward me, I felt an ache in my chest, as if my heart were breaking. *How can I leave them?* I asked myself. *How can I help them understand what is happening?* I did not understand myself. I was no longer able to provide the love and attention that my daughters needed and deserved, and my spirit was heavy with guilt.

Being a wife and mother meant everything to me. I had never pursued a career because I wanted to give all I had to my family. I wanted to focus my energy on them. The problem was that I no longer had any energy. I had nothing left to give.

One year earlier I had believed my life was perfect. Lying in the hospital room, holding my newborn daughter, I experienced an overwhelming sense of peace and joy, unlike anything I had ever felt before. I had a wonderful husband, Tim, two beautiful children, and more blessings than I had ever hoped for. *What had happened?*

On this dreary morning, just days after baby Jenna's first birthday, I realized that my fairy-tale life had fallen apart. Instead of looking forward to each new day, I dreaded waking up. I had lost the desire to play with my children. Lying on the couch *watching* them play was the best that I could do. I used to love talking to my girls, telling them stories and listening to Lauren's chatter, but even the sound of their voices had become irritating. I no longer wanted to talk, to listen, or to answer anyone's questions. I just wanted to be alone.

None of my previous hobbies or activities held any interest for me anymore. I didn't want to leave the house or my bed. All I wanted to do was sleep—eternally, if possible.

Death seemed like the only avenue to peace. When I expressed these feelings to my physician, he was alarmed. I was referred to a psychiatrist the very next day, who diagnosed me with major clinical depression, prescribed an antidepressant medication, and recommended that I be hospitalized for my own protection. My life took a U-turn of major proportion as I went home to pack a few essentials for my hospital stay and to say good-bye to my children. It was the first of many good-byes to follow.

Walking down the long hallway toward the psychiatric ward, I sensed with each step I took that I was losing a piece of myself. As the door closed behind me, I felt defeated and confused. *What's someone like me doing in a place like this?* I wondered.

After a nurse had shown me to my room, Tim returned. He had just met with my psychiatrist. "The doctor said the medication will help you feel better in a couple of weeks. Then you'll be able to come home," my husband told me as he sat next to me on the tiny bed. I felt relieved by this news. *Two weeks isn't such a long time,* I thought. But the doctor was wrong. Two weeks stretched into eight months, and that was just my *first* hospitalization.

In the years that followed, I spent more than 80 weeks in hospital psychiatric wards. Twenty different medications were prescribed, and I received 200 electroconvulsive treatments (shock treatments).

Depression is a strange illness. Most terminally ill people have a spirit that longs to live, even though the body is dying. As a depressed person, I felt that my spirit had already died, and my body just refused to follow it to the grave. I was torn between my desire to end my own suffering and the knowledge that in so doing I would be leaving a legacy of incredible pain and sorrow for my daughters and my husband. My choice to live was not easy on them either.

My children had to deal with the reality of having a mother who could not care for them. My husband had a partner who was unable to contribute anything to the marriage. Tim became my caregiver and parented our daughters alone, making a conscious effort to provide them with the affection, support, and love that they needed. He did his job well.

People often asked Tim, "How do you do it?" There were some people who said they would not be so patient, so sacrificial. Many people saw him as a pillar of strength, but Tim didn't feel very strong. No one knew about the nights when he quietly slipped into an empty church and sat in a pew, weeping and praying that God would give him strength and heal me. My husband became my lifeline of intercessory prayer to God on my behalf. Years later he confessed to me how afraid he was. "I used to dread coming home from work. When I opened the door, I didn't know if you would still be there, and if you were, I didn't know if you would be alive," he said.

The years of my depression were frightening but also very lonely for Tim. The woman he had married was gone. He once told me, "I used to see couples together, holding hands and smiling, and I wondered, *Why can't I have someone like that—a wife who smiles?*"

I have wondered about the timing of my depression. It stole some of the most important years of my life. Why couldn't it have happened before I was married, before I had children who needed a mother? Now I realize the wisdom of God's timing. I do not believe that I would have been able to endure this devastating illness on my own. In my children, God gave me someone to live for, when I no longer wanted to go on. In my husband, God gave me the strength I needed to get through each day.

Tim's response to my illness was a key factor in my surviving depression. He was always there to provide the encouragement and support that I needed. Many times I would call him at work, hysterical with fear. "I can't live like this anymore! I am so scared!" I would cry. Tim would drop whatever he was doing and be by my side in a matter of minutes. As my husband held me, he assured me, "Everything will be all right. You *will* get better." I believed him when he told me, "No matter what happens, I will always love you. I will never leave you." In my soul I knew that when I could no longer push forward, Tim would be there to carry me.

After nine years, my diagnosis was changed to "refractory" depression—depression that does not respond to treatment. It became apparent that the cure I desperately needed would not come through medical treatment.

While at home, I began to see a Christian counselor. Together, as believers in Christ, "Berys" and I invited the Holy Spirit into each counseling session. He revealed much to me.

In the months that followed, I learned that the roots of my depression were not biochemical or emotional, but *spiritual*. I discovered lies that I had believed my entire life, which had led to my depression. I was not the worthless person I had always thought I was. I was a beloved child of the King! This truth and others transformed my life. Three months after my psychiatrist's grim diagnosis, I was healed.

I never returned to the psychiatric ward. I never received another shock treatment. I no longer needed medication or the care of a psychiatrist. Six years have passed, and I remain free from depression! Tim and I are enjoying this second chance we have been given to experience life and marriage.

Recently I asked my husband what made him remain faithful to me during those dark years. His reply was very honest: "While you were sick, it didn't really seem like we had a marriage relationship, so I just kept telling myself you were my 'mission field,' my ministry opportunity." Tim humbly credits God for giving him the strength to do the right thing, for answering his prayers when prayers were all he had to give.

And me? God answered my prayers in healing me, He answered my prayers in getting my children through the ordeal, and He answered my prayers in countless other ways. But Scripture tells us, "The greatest of these is love," and it was the unconditional love of my husband that was the greatest answered prayer of it all. I thank God each day for giving me Tim.

Divorce can be devastating for everyone involved, especially for the spouse who feels he or she has been terribly wronged. Yet it is not enough to pray for answers if we are too stubborn to listen to what the Lord is telling us. Only when we come humbly before Him in repentance for our own sin can true healing take place. Karen found out she would never be free until she freed herself from the bitter pain of unforgiveness.

The Healing Power of Forgiveness

BY KAREN O'CONNOR, SAN DIEGO, CALIFORNIA

I thought about her. I dreamed about her. I saw her in every woman I met. Some had her name: Cathy. Other women had her deep-set blue eyes or curly, dark hair. Even the slightest resemblance turned my stomach into a knot.

Weeks, months, years passed. Was I never to be free of this woman who had gone after my husband, Jack, then following our divorce had married him? The resentment, guilt, and anger drained the life out of everything I did. I went into counseling. I attended self-help classes, enrolled in seminars and workshops. I read books. I talked to anyone who would listen.

I ran. I walked the beach. I drove for miles to nowhere. I screamed into my pillow at night. I prayed. I blamed myself. I did everything I knew how to do—except surrender. *How could this have happened?* I asked myself over and over.

I had been happy before she came into my life. At least I thought I was. My days were simple, predictable, and filled with good things— the stuff most women long for: a successful husband, children I loved, tennis with my friends three mornings a week, church on Sundays, summer vacations, a lovely home, and a beautiful car. What more could I have wanted?

Suddenly everything was different. My life would never be the same again. I did not like what I saw in myself. I hated this woman. And I was beginning to hate the man I had loved for over 20 years—my husband, the father of my children. *How can any good come from such pain and grief?* I asked myself over and over.

I did not receive an answer right away. But I know now that God did have a response, which occurred to me one Saturday when I was drawn to a day-long seminar on the healing power of forgiveness held at a church in my neighborhood. After the introduction, some discussion, and sharing, the leader invited participants to close their eyes and locate someone in their lives they had not forgiven for whatever reason, real or imagined. Cathy's name loomed large in my mind.

Next he asked whether or not we would be willing to forgive that person. My stomach churned again. My hands were suddenly wet, and my head throbbed. I felt I had to get out of that room, but something kept me in my seat.

How could I forgive a person like Cathy? She had hurt not only me, but she had also hurt my children. I turned my attention to other people in my life. My mother—she would be easy to forgive, or my friend Ann, or my former high school English teacher. Anyone except Cathy. But there was no escape. The name persisted, and the image of her face in my mind would not fade.

Then a voice within gently asked, "Are you ready to let go of this, to release her? To forgive yourself as well?" It was not an audible voice, but rather an impression. I knew it was the Holy Spirit pursuing me.

I turned hot, then cold. I began to shake. I was certain everyone around me could hear my heart beating. Yes, I was willing. I could not hold on to my anger any longer. It was killing me. In that moment, without doing anything else, an incredible shift occurred within. I simply let go!

I cannot describe it. In that moment I was suddenly willing to do something I had doggedly resisted for years. For the first time since my husband had left, I gave control of my life to the Holy Spirit. I released my grip on Cathy, on Jack, on myself. I let go of the rage and resentment—just like that.

Within seconds, energy rushed through every cell of my body. My mind became alert, my heart lightened. Suddenly I realized that as long as I separate myself from even one person, I separate myself from God.

How self-righteous I had been, how judgmental. How important it had been for me to be right, no matter what the cost. And it had cost me plenty: my health, my spontaneity, my aliveness, my relationship with God.

I had no idea what would occur next, but it did not matter. That night I slept straight through till morning. No dreams. No haunting face. No reminders.

If it had been up to me alone, I don't know if I would have had the courage or the generosity to make the first move. But it was not up to me. There was no mistaking the power of the Holy Spirit within me.

The following Monday I walked into my office and wrote Cathy a letter. The words spilled onto the page without effort.

"Dear Cathy," I began. "On Saturday morning…" I proceeded to tell her what had occurred during the seminar. I also told her how I had hated her for what she had done to my marriage and to my family and, as a result, how I had denied both of us the healing power of forgiveness. I apologized for my hateful thoughts. I signed my name, slipped the letter into an envelope, and popped it in the mailbox without looking back.

On Wednesday afternoon of the same week, the phone rang.

"Karen?"

There was no mistaking the voice.

"It's Cathy," she said softly.

I was surprised that my stomach remained calm. My hands were dry. My voice was steady and sure. I listened more than I talked—unusual for me. I found myself actually interested in what Cathy had to say.

She thanked me for the letter, and she acknowledged my courage in writing it. Then she told me how sorry she was for everything. She talked briefly about her regret, her sadness for me, for my children, and more. All I had ever wanted to hear from her, she said that day.

As I replaced the receiver, however, another insight came to me. I realized that as nice as it was to hear her words of apology, they paled in comparison to what God was teaching me. Buried deep in the trauma of my divorce was the truth that I had been looking for all my life without even knowing it. God is my Source, my Strength, my very Supply. He alone can bring about restoration.

Clearly, God was answering my prayer for healing—healing from hateful thoughts, healing from restless nights of torment, healing from the powerlessness I felt over my life.

For four years I had been caught in the externals, the reasons, the lies, the excuses, the jealousy, the anger. But now I had a clear experience of what until then had been a stack of psychological insights. I really knew that no one can hurt me as long as I am in God's hands. No one can rob me of my joy unless I allow it.

My life is mine. Every experience, no matter how painful or confusing, can serve my spiritual growth. Every moment has its purpose if I am serving the Lord.

Since then I have started over again in another city, joined a church where I am welcome, and have remarried. My husband, Charles, is truly an answer to my prayer for a Christian husband who is my partner in all things. I am now free of the binding ties of jealousy, anger, and resentment—free to experience all that God has for me. My children are healing, and we are beginning to laugh again. Yes, I thought I was happy when I lived that shallow, predictable life, but now I know what true happiness is: walking one step at a time behind the Great Shepherd who leads me on the paths He has chosen.

"'For I know the plans I have for you,' says the LORD, 'plans to prosper you and not to harm you, plans to give you hope and a future'" (Jeremiah 29:11-12). And He has done just that through answered prayer.

> Married life is never without its struggles. To keep a family together takes plenty of work and plenty of prayer. Jennifer and Troy learned how much the power of prayer could help when they found themselves and their marriage in trouble.

For Better or Worse... with Boxing Gloves and Running Shoes

BY JENNIFER S. MCMAHAN, AMARILLO, TEXAS

After nine years of marriage, my husband, Troy, hastily backed out of the driveway and drove off with the contents of his closet. I stood at the front door, angry, crying, and totally lost. We had had an argument—*another* argument. It was a scene we had repeated many times. This time, however, it felt different. Troy left. It felt final.

I fell to my knees and clutched my two-and-a-half-year-old daughter.

"Why did Daddy leave?" she asked.

"We'll be okay, honey," was all I could say.

Scooping her up into my arms, I walked into the nursery to check on her baby sister. The life I had envisioned for my girls was crumbling around us. Troy and I had married young. At first we lived in a rather modest apartment with our dog, Dan, and were completely in love. One of our favorite things to do was get away for the weekend. When school and work were through for the week, we would head out of town and stay away until late Sunday. Dan went on every trip. The three of us were a little family. During long drives, we would plan our future and solve the world's problems. Communication came easily for us, as long as we did not disagree.

Marriage took us by surprise. It was a lot harder than we had imagined. In the area of conflict resolution we failed miserably. Troy had no idea how to deal with conflict—a failing he came by naturally. His parents divorced after 30 years of unresolved conflict and resentment.

Me? I entered the marriage without thinking twice about breaking into a full-fledged, screaming confrontation. It worked when I was growing up—and my family was close! We each brought something of our past to the marriage. Troy brought his running shoes, and I brought a megaphone and boxing gloves.

Both Troy and I were brought up in Christian homes, but neither of us had a real relationship with Christ. We didn't even attend church. Satan slowly and discretely slipped into the heart of our marriage very early and began his destruction. Even so, Troy and I had many good times. After a while though, the repetitive fighting and arguing took their toll. The bad began to outweigh the good. We started to grow distant. Our fights went on for hours into the night.

Every time we would begin to grow close, a terrible argument would sever the connection between us.

Pride fueled our problem. Neither of us wanted to admit we had marital problems. Unfortunately, hiding from them did not make our problems go away. It was like having a body overrun with cancer and not visiting the doctor. As a result, we erected thicker walls of resentment between us year after year.

Eventually, we became part of a terrific church group, and their support helped a little. We would sit side by side on Sunday morning, just like the other couples, but we were merely pretending to be a happily married couple.

So there I was after nine years of marriage, watching my husband drive away. I had two choices at that point. I could change the locks and find a lawyer, or I could swallow my pride, make some changes, and call for help. Panic set in immediately. I had to pull my marriage back together, for myself and for my two precious babies. I did not want my stubbornness or selfishness causing my girls to grow up toting a suitcase to their father's house every other weekend. I wanted our marriage to work. So I discarded my pride and called for help. I called almost everyone I was close to: family, church friends, nonchurch friends, my parents, Troy's grandmother. We needed help or the relationship was over for good.

"Amazing" is the only way I can describe what happened after everyone began to pray. It was as if God said, "All you had to do was ask." My parents came to help me with my girls and to be there for me. Church friends left their own families to be with Troy. He had been feeling the same desperation as I was and had called on people as well.

One of the most significant blessings in our lives was his job. Troy told the owners of his company about the trouble in his marriage. They stopped to pray with him right there at work! Praise the Lord for Christian leaders in the workplace! Within hours of admitting we needed help, my husband and I were surrounded in prayer. It was difficult to expose the ugliness in our life. We looked like such a perfect little family, but God truly worked on our situation through the intercessory prayers of those who loved us.

During the course of the next couple of days, Troy and I met with a special mediator—a person who loves both of us a great deal: my dad. He talked, he listened, and he was able to be objective in helping us work through things. Later, my mom told me how my dad had prayed before meeting with us, asking God to guide his words and to speak through him. He told my mom there were times when he did not know what was going to come out of his mouth until he heard himself say the words. My husband and I agreed to work things out. The Spirit of the Lord was there with us, mending our hearts back together.

Years of resentment take a long time to heal. The wounds seem to always be right under the skin, but we made a commitment to each other and agreed that divorce would not be an option. Without prayer, a loving family, and friends to surround us, we would be packing up our girls every other weekend and sending them back and forth between two separate houses. I praise God that we are conquering Satan in this struggle. The power of prayer is tremendous. We still have conflict, but our ground rules have totally changed. We have ditched the boxing gloves, megaphone, and running shoes. God is the head of our marriage now, and all because of the power of prayer.

How often in your life have you felt the need to pray for a friend? When God places the need on your heart to help intercede for someone, do not believe it doesn't matter. Your friend may only know something is missing in life, or the person may know what he or she needs, but not how to ask for it. It can be your prayer that helps pull your friend through. It was just such a friend's prayer that brought Anna just what she needed.

What Does Anna Need?

BY SANDRA MCGARRITY, CHESAPEAKE, VIRGINIA

A beautiful, young woman with her honey-colored hair and expressive eyes, she moved with feminine grace and spoke softly. She was kind and hardworking. For the sake of her privacy, I am going to call her "Anna."

"Why," I asked myself, "would a man be unfaithful to a wife like her?"

By the time I met Anna at our church day care where we both worked, she had already survived the divorce. She didn't elaborate on the story and didn't dwell on it in her daily life. Someone told me Anna had come home one day to find her husband not with another woman, but with another man.

Anna came to work every day with her less-than-a-year-old son perched on one arm, towing her three-year-old son with the other hand, and somehow managing to lug along a purse, diaper bag, and three lunches. I never heard her complain. In fact, she showed up in much the same manner to all of the church services. She willingly took her turn serving in the church nursery. She took full responsibility for providing a home for her children.

One Sunday night she came for prayer during the church service. As the wife of the assistant pastor, I was often called upon to pray with someone. On that night, the pastor silently signaled for me to come pray with her.

"What can I pray with you for?" I asked her.

She was in tears. "I don't mean to complain," she began, "but life is so hard. I feel so alone. I don't know what to do."

I calmly answered, "Let's pray." Inwardly I did some hasty praying of my own. "Help me, Lord! What should I pray for? What does Anna need?"

The answer came to me immediately. It was not a voice or a vision, but I knew in my heart what I had to pray for. Still I hesitated. "What if my prayer isn't right?" Worse than that, I might make myself look foolish.

I had hesitated for as long as I could. I had to do something. I had to plunge in. "Father, Anna is alone. We know that You care for her. She has been so faithful in her life. I believe that she needs a good husband to share her life and to help her. We are asking tonight that You give Anna a husband. Amen."

She arose from prayer with a radiant smile. I arose a little stunned about what I had prayed, but somehow at peace.

A week later, our pastor announced in the service that one of our local navy men had suffered an eye injury in an accident on his ship. He asked that we pray for this young man. I joined the congregation in prayer for his recovery.

Anna put feet to her prayers. She visited him in the hospital several times. A friendship grew between them. After his time in the hospital, he attended church regularly, and they began sitting together during services. The friendship quickly blossomed into romance. I was surprised, but Anna did not seem to be at all surprised. Within a few months they were married.

He was a wonderful husband to her and a good father to her children. A year later they added a third son to the family and moved away to a larger apartment. They eventually moved to another state when his time with the navy was finished.

I have lost touch with her, but I will never forget God's love for that single mother. I enjoyed seeing them become a little family. I enjoyed the feeling of knowing the Lord answered my humble prayer and gave Anna a new start.

8
God and the "Little Things" in Life

Sometimes we make the mistake of thinking prayers should only be for the "big" things in life: a serious illness, financial provision, a broken relationship. But for God there are truly no "little" things. Jesus tells us that the very hairs on our head are numbered. If God has time to count the hairs on our head, then truly there can be nothing that matters to us that does not also matter to God.

The following stories show God's hand in seemingly small matters. But to the people who prayed, they were not small at all. And neither were these things small to God as He abundantly answered each request.

In all of our lives come the small things that bother us. Never hesitate to take even the most insignificant request to God.

If you care, He cares.

> *I have told you these things, so that in me you may have peace. In this world you will have trouble. But take heart! I have overcome the world* (John 16:33)....

In each of us there lies an unfulfilled dream—something we
have been too afraid to try because we fear failure. B. J. never
gave up on her dream, even when the odds were against her.
No prayer is too great or difficult for the Lord. Just ask and He
can make your dreams come true, just as He did for B. J.

Dance for Me

BY B. J. JENSEN, SAN DIEGO, CALIFORNIA

As a child, I dreamed of becoming an entertainer who could sing,
dance, and act. Ironically, I sang so far off-key that people within
earshot cringed. I was born crippled and contracted polio at age ten,
so I was obviously "dancing challenged," but that didn't lessen my
prayers. I longed to take the necessary lessons, but my parents were
not cooperative. They dismissed my appeals because our family could
not afford such luxuries as dance lessons. And so my stifled childhood aspirations were packed up and put on the dusty back shelf.

Half a century later my subdued, creative caterpillar emerged from
its cocoon, raring to go. Joyfully I accepted a paid position to develop
and direct a drama program at our church! I felt honored, yet somewhat intimidated, because I lacked the formal drama education.

As my fifty-second birthday approached, friends enticed me to
join them at the annual Christian Artists' Seminar in the Rockies,
where thousands of Christian artists assembled for competition,
training, and nightly entertainment by top-notch celebrities.

My spirit soared. Perhaps this was my opportunity to learn from
experienced Christian drama professionals. But there was one major
obstacle: finances.

I prayed, "Lord, if it is Your will for this flower bud to blossom,
I will need Your financial fertilizer!" Within the week, I received

unexpected checks that provided the total sum of all expenses! I dropped to my knees in gratitude. "God, I am so overwhelmed with Your generosity. Since You've opened this door of opportunity, what is Your plan for me?"

I was not prepared for the immediate response I perceived in my mind: *"Dance for Me."* My hesitation produced a louder echo in my heart: *"Dance for Me in the competition."*

I didn't get it. My limited dancing experiences were confined to the privacy of my own living room. The thought of dancing in public at my age and size was almost comical. "I do want to be obedient, Lord, but I'm terrified!"

Encouragement from family and friends boosted my disbelief. Maybe this was something I *could* do. I continued to pray and felt inspired to choreograph a dance routine for the upcoming competition. Then off I flew to Colorado for the conference.

The transition from sea level in San Diego to 8500 feet in the Rockies was breathtaking in more ways than one. The grandeur of the snow-capped Rocky Mountains against the crystal-clear blue sky was magnificent. Estes Park scenery was reminiscent of a picturesque travel brochure displaying sparkling lakes and promising tall, fragrant pine trees. It seemed like paradise.

Monday morning, I faced my dance competitors. Most were teenagers. Watching their warm-ups, I realized they were so accomplished they must have danced out of the womb! Dressed in their cute leotards, they executed exquisite dance moves I didn't even know existed! My dream of competing was turning into a nightmare.

The four judges for the competition were talented professional dancers. They offered three-minute constructive critiques at the end of each competitor's routine. I felt out of my league as I waited for my turn in the back of the auditorium dressed in a makeshift costume recycled from old, sheer beige curtains.

When my name was called, I timidly stepped forward, trying unsuccessfully to hide my half-century-old physique. *What am I doing here?* I screamed internally. *I am totally out of my comfort zone. I really have to swallow my pride to dance for You in public, Lord!*

My music started. I danced. The music ended.

As I waited vulnerably alone on the dance floor for the judges to confer, the crocodiles of doubt and discouragement surrounded me and nipped at my heels.

The head judge finally rose after what seemed like an eternity. With trepidation, I braced myself for the evaluation. Her silence pounded in my ears. Eventually she whispered ever so softly, "Awesome."

The intended compliment could not penetrate the murky swamp of self-imposed misery. Was she trying to be kind to an old lady who just showed up? Weren't the judges going to acknowledge my courage and effort? My face turned bright-red with humiliation as I lowered my head and dejectedly slipped away from the dance floor.

Dance competitors were then instructed to attend *all* dance classes offered during the week for eligibility in the competition. I was distressed, deflated, and downcast. The dance and drama classes occurred at the same times! I wanted to do what God asked of me, but it was becoming very inconvenient!

With hot tears of discouragement, I decided it would be better to drop out of the dance competition instead of perpetuating this charade. Then I would be free to attend the drama training. I hoped God would understand that sometimes what He asks of us is just too difficult and too sacrificial.

Again a strong, persistent request filled my head: *"Dance for Me."*

Halfheartedly, I surrendered.

Participating in the required dance classes stretched not only my ability level, but also my limbs into unfamiliar and uncomfortable contortions. By midweek, muscles I had not heard from in years threatened to revolt completely.

Half-conscious because of exhaustion, I slumped in my seat at Thursday evening's concert. Something I heard when the emcee announced the competition finalists caused me to sit bolt upright. My name! Was it a mistake…or a miracle? It didn't matter. At least now I could tell all who had provided financial support, prayers, and encouragement that their belief in me was not totally wasted!

In my room before the final competition on Friday, my heart overflowed with gratitude. "Thank You, Lord, for answered prayers. For the first time in my life, I feel like a dancer. Is there anything else I can do for You?"

An immediate response filled my being: "*Dance for Me…without your wig.*" Horror gripped my heart, and I recoiled as if struck by a rattlesnake. "I'd feel naked without my wig, Lord. I couldn't go out in public feeling so vulnerable and exposed. Anything…anything but that! *Please* don't ask that of me!" My pleas were followed by complete silence.

I had worn a wig for 17 years. Tumor surgery and two heart attacks in 1980 caused my ample head of curly, reddish hair to fall out in clumps. The sparse, ash-gray straight hair that grew back was embarrassing. The thought of going anywhere without my "security blanket" was paralyzing and more than I thought I could bear.

Overwhelming turmoil consumed me because I did not understand. Why would God continue to ask the impossible of me? "*Trust in the Lord with all your heart and lean not on your own understanding,*" flashed through my mind. I wanted to trust, to be obedient, but I was definitely wrestling.

Finally spent, I relented. I traded the most difficult gifts I could give God: *my* will and pride for submission, trust, and obedience. I would return home transformed and a winner, no matter what the outcome of the competition. Slowly I removed my wig and in naked humility headed to the final competition.

Excitement escalated during the finals of dance, vocal, instrumental, writing, and drama competitions in Estes Park. I did my best to dance for God and left the outcome in His hands. Winners of the coveted and prestigious awards were to be announced at the final concert that evening.

When the competitions ended, I felt a great sense of relief and silently declared my commitment fulfilled. I had given the best I had to give. I was leaving the auditorium with my head up this time.

The head judge approached me saying, "Love your new hairdo, B.J. Great job." Because of my changed attitude, for the first time in 50 years, I did not feel embarrassed or apologetic for my looks or dancing inadequacies.

The judge went on to say, "It is my privilege to tell you the judges have unanimously voted you the dance-competition winner!" In my numbness, all I could think of was, "Thank You, God, for answered prayer." *"Whoever humbles himself will be exalted."*

Then the topper: "You have also been selected the grand-prize winner of all the arts competitions. You'll dance in the closing concert tonight. Congratulations on a most inspiring routine!"

Tears gushed from my eyes as "my cup runneth over." I could not believe it! God heard the prayers of this tone-deaf, crippled child and rewarded my obedience, courage, and trust far beyond my wildest dreams.

That night, this liberated grandma with "au natural" hair appeared center stage, in front of the other 600 contestants and 3000 spectators, to dance my testimony about rising above life's circumstances and limitations. What an incredible mountaintop experience!

"Here, Lord, this dance is for You!"

Many of us have had a job situation that required a major move. Many of us know what it feels like to face an unknown situation in an unknown town. We should never be afraid to pray for exactly what we are looking for. Suzan knew exactly what she wanted and asked the Lord to provide.

God and the Map

BY SUZAN STRADER, COTO DE CAZA, CALIFORNIA

Facedown, flat on the floor, a map of the country at my head, my left hand covered the western states as I prayed, "God, please give my husband a job!"

It had been 18 long months since Joe's sudden unemployment, and each day was longer than the one before. Somewhere in the midst of it all, I began this daily ritual of prayer.

Would the next move take us to the northeast? The southwest? The North Pole? I had no idea where God wanted us, but I was willing to go anywhere He chose. I *did* have a preference though (in case God wanted to know). My large family still lived in Southern California, the place I had grown up. Although we loved it here in Kentucky, I would not mind at all being back in the Golden State.

Job possibilities throughout the United States played with my imagination like summer thunderstorm clouds in a drought, evaporating just as quickly. Several times I mentally packed our house for places I had only heard of, just to find out that it was not to be. Now I dared ask God to give us a job within a day's drive of any of my siblings.

As one door opened and another slammed shut in our faces, ritual became important to me. It symbolized the longings of my heart. Day after day, down on the floor I went, the familiar atlas open, left hand over the "Left Coast" of the country. I prayed like this for months.

One evening Joe stepped carefully over me and the atlas as he reached for the phone.

"Finally I've reached you!" said the voice on the other end. "I've been calling all over the country. What are you doing now?"

Wondering what this was leading up to, Joe responded, "I'm doing some consulting. How about you?"

"You won't believe it, but I'm back in Southern California, running a couple of facilities. I have a big problem with one of them, and you're the only person I know who can solve it," he said. "Would you be available to fly to Southern California for some consulting work?"

Would he be available!

My husband was on a plane very soon after that conversation. Three weeks later, as the problem was nearing resolution, it looked like the job search would be on again. Would Joe consider doing a bit more work for that company? the man asked. That was in May. By September we had a contract for permanent employment.

Wow! Isn't God great? We could say that now, but what about my attitude during the waiting period? Was God also great then? I am the first to admit that I had my days of frustration, disappointment, and yes, even doubt. But God, being the constant, perfect Being that He is, was on the job 24/7. I had no idea what He had planned as I spent those hours praying. But I knew I could trust Him because He keeps His promises. He promised never to leave or forsake me. Trust is the basis of any relationship, and God asks for a high level of trust as we grow in relationship with Him.

The house we purchased was only a handful of miles from where we had lived for 20 years prior to our move to Kentucky. It was an easy drive to visit most of my family. It was also right under my left hand when I prayed over the map on the floor!

Of course, I also prayed for insight for what I should do with my time. Obedience is a big thing with God. He expects His children to obey Him. We often get this backward, thinking we can become worthy of His blessings by obeying Him. The Bible says God blesses us regardless! We are to obey Him as a result of His blessing us, not to cause His blessings. Along with the comfortable and familiar surroundings, the move also meant a new teaching ministry for me. As an experienced Bible teacher, I was asked to head a start-up branch of a national organization.

Thinking back over that long season of fervent prayer, I see many results and benefits I would not have experienced unless God had grabbed my attention through our need. I am so glad He heard and saw me on the floor with my hand on the map! Now I know He had the move planned all along. He just wanted me to see it, too.

God often has His own time period to test our desire, trust, and commitment. If we continue doing what we know is right, He takes notice. It may not turn out the way we think it should, but it will turn out God's way—which, after all, is the best way for us.

It is easy to get caught up in the busyness of life and forget the peaceful beauty of the world around us. Nancy got a wake-up call one busy day when she realized God had been talking to her all along. All she had to do was stop long enough to listen to His voice.

Be Still with God

BY NANCY B. GIBBS, CORDELE, GEORGIA

All day long, I had been very busy. Picking up trash, cleaning bathrooms, and scrubbing floors were all on my agenda for the day. My grown children were coming home for the weekend, and I wanted everything to be perfect. Ribs and chicken awaited my grill, and all the shopping was done.

Suddenly, I realized how dog-tired I was. I simply could not work as long as I used to be able to when I was younger. "I've got to rest for a minute," I told my husband, Roy, as I collapsed into my favorite rocking chair. Music was playing, my cat and dog were chasing each other around, and the phone interrupted my quiet.

A Scripture from Psalms came to mind: "Be still, and know that I am God" (Psalm 46:10). I realized that I had not spent much time in prayer that day. Was I too busy to even utter a simple word of thanks to God? The thought of my beautiful patio came to mind. *I can be quiet out there.* I longed for a few minutes alone with my Savior.

Roy and I had invested a great deal of time and work into our patio that spring, and the flowers and hanging baskets were breathtaking. It was definitely a place of tranquillity and rest. *If I can't be still with God out there, I can't be still anywhere.* I slipped out the back door while Roy was on the phone and sat down in my favorite patio chair. I closed my eyes and began to pray.

A bird flew by, singing a beautiful song, and landed on the feeder. I watched as it began to eat dinner. After a few minutes, it flew off, singing as it went.

I closed my eyes again, and a gust of wind blew, causing my wind chimes to dance. They made a joyful sound, but again, I lost my concentration. I looked up toward the blue sky and watched the clouds moving slowly toward the horizon. The wind died down, and my chimes stopped their song.

Again I bowed my head. "Honk, honk!" I almost jumped out of my skin. A neighbor was driving down the street, waving and smiling at me as he passed by. I waved back, happy he cared, but tried to settle back down again.

I repeated the familiar verse in my mind. *Be still, and know that I am God.*

"I'm trying, God. I really am," I whispered. "But You've got to help me here."

The back door opened and my husband walked outside. "I was wondering where you were." He bent down to kiss my cheek. "I love you."

I chuckled and watched him turn to walk back inside. *He didn't know where I was and just had to check on me?*

"Where's the quiet time, Lord?" My heart began to flutter. No pain, but another brief distraction. *This is impossible. There's no time to be still. There's too much going on in the world and entirely too much activity around me.*

And then suddenly, it dawned on me. God was speaking to me the entire time I was attempting to be still. "Thank You for the joy of music," I remember saying at the beginning of my quiet time, and He sent a sparrow to lighten my life with song. "Thank You for the comfortable world You created, Lord." And He sent a gentle breeze. "Thank You for my friends." And a neighbor drove by, catching my attention with a honk of his horn. And then I thanked Him for my family. He, in turn, sent my sweetheart to offer his sentiments of love.

"Thank You, Father, for life." And He caused my heart to flutter. *Thank You, Lord, for counting my blessings along with me, and multiplying them along the way.*

9
On Foreign Soil

"Blessed is the nation whose God is the LORD" (Psalm 33:12). This is the message we need to take to our neighboring countries and foreign lands. Thousands of missionaries, dedicated to accomplishing great things for God, toil in distant lands. Our daily prayers require inclusion of these dedicated people and their families.

In addition to praying for our missionaries, we also need to pray for God's Word to become known in foreign and international lands. God can and will work through the inhabitants of the nations that honor and serve Him. Psalm 34:8 says, "Taste and see that the LORD is good; blessed is the man who takes refuge in him." Let us pray that every nation on earth will take refuge in God and hear His Word.

For, as Paul assures us, faith comes by hearing. Today's missionaries walk the same road as that of the apostle. Mission workers experience life from his perspective. It takes courage and boldness to proclaim the gospel in areas where death could be the result of sharing God's love. Those involved in missions know that faith comes by hearing! And protection for those in the field is strengthened by those at home praying!

> *Do you not know? Have you not heard? The LORD is the everlasting God, the Creator of the ends of the earth. He will not grow tired or weary, and his understanding no one can fathom* (Isaiah 40:28).

Most of us, by the grace of God, have not endured the separation from a loved one due to war. Not because they are serving in the military, but because they are being hunted by opposing forces. Renie prayed for the Lord to unite her grandfather with her and her grandmother. It took some time, but the Lord answered.

The Voice of God

by Renie Szilak Burghardt, Doniphan, Missouri

Throughout the years of World War II in our country of Hungary, somehow my grandparents, who were raising me, and I managed to survive, although we had many close calls. But when that terrible war finally ended in 1945, there was no jubilation for the people of Hungary, because Soviet troops occupied the land now, holding our country hostage in the arms of Communism. Suddenly, people who spoke out against new oppressions that began to take place were rounded up by the newly formed secret-police force and never seen again!

My grandfather, a retired judge, was not afraid to speak out, and one day, in the fall of 1945, two men appeared at our house to take him away. They said he was being taken in for questioning only. Grandfather, pointing out that his hands were dirty from working in the garden, asked the men if he could wash up first. The men agreed. When he did not come out of the bathroom within a few minutes, the men ran and pushed the door open. The water in the sink was still running, but Grandfather had disappeared! He had managed to jump out the bathroom window and flee on foot. The two men raced out the door and up and down our street, looking for Grandfather, while my grandmother held me close, as we tearfully prayed to God to keep Grandpa safe from harm.

Grandfather managed to elude capture and went into hiding, while life became more and more difficult for Grandmother and me. We lived on soup made from a few vegetables that grew in our garden, and we never knew when the secret police would show up at our house again in hopes of finding Grandpa. Sometimes they came in the middle of the night, breaking down our door. Fear became our constant companion then, but prayer was what kept us hanging on.

For two years my grandfather eluded capture, and although at times he sent word to us that he was safe, most of the time we did not know his whereabouts. Grandmother and I missed him terribly. The thought that we might never be together again upset me, and I constantly prayed that we could be reunited. But on an autumn day in 1947, when I was almost ten years old, I knew exactly where to find him, and it seemed as though the time had come for us to be reunited.

The day before, new elections were held in our country, and I waited for the results with hope in my heart. So the morning after the elections when our radio announced that the Communist party had been defeated, I was overjoyed! Celebrations erupted in the streets, too, with none of us realizing that the Communist government, backed by the Soviet troops, was not about to give up power, elections or no elections.

But after listening to the radio broadcast, my ten-year-old mind concluded the election results meant that Grandfather could come home and we could be a family again. I immediately wondered if Grandfather, who we recently learned was hiding out on a nearby farm, had heard the good news. I decided now was a good time to hike out to the farm and tell him. Then we could come home together and surprise Grandma! Of course, I did not tell her of my plan. Instead of going to school, I set out for Grandfather's hiding place. As I reached the outskirts of our village without drawing any attention to myself, anticipation filled my heart. In a short while I would see

Grandfather for the first time in over two years, and we would walk home together and live as a family again. My eyes filled with tears of joy at that thought, and I began to walk faster.

Suddenly, I was startled when I heard a man's voice calling my name. I stopped dead in my tracks and looked all around me, but saw no one.

"Who are you? Where are you? I can't see you," I asked, straining to see if the speaker might be behind some nearby bushes.

"It isn't important where I am," the voice said. "I am here to warn you that you are about to put your grandfather in grave danger, for you are being followed. Turn around and go back to your grandmother immediately, and know that you will all be together soon."

Of course, very frightened now, I immediately turned and began running back toward the village, my heart pounding so hard I thought it would jump right out of my chest. I ran past a man on a bicycle and recognized him as one of the secret police that had been at our house. I was being followed!

Reaching our house, I found Grandma outside pacing back and forth in the street.

"Oh, thank God, you are all right!" she cried, gathering me in her arms. "They came to tell me that you were not in school, and I thought someone had taken you away."

"I decided to go and tell Grandfather that the Communists lost the election," I wailed. "I thought we could come home together and surprise you!"

"Oh my!" Grandma said, shaking her head. "Oh my!"

"But someone stopped me," I continued excitedly, tears streaming down my face. "A voice told me I was being followed and that I should run back home. It was the kindest, most loving voice I have ever heard, Grandma. I think it was the voice of God speaking to me. No one else knew of my plan!"

My grandmother nodded silently, ushered me into the house, and while holding me close, reassured me that everything would be better soon.

Two weeks later, a man came to get us in the middle of the night. By the time the sun rose, we had traveled many miles to a place near the Austrian border where a large group of ethnic Germans were about to be deported into Austria. My heart leapt with joy when I saw Grandfather there. He looked into my eyes lovingly and hugged me tightly. We were to be smuggled out of our country as ethnic Germans. Aware of the danger still around us, we did not dare breathe a sigh of relief until we crossed the border. In Austria we ended up in a refugee camp along with hundreds of other destitute refugees, but at least we were finally together again as a family.

Grandfather remained fearful that the long arm of Communism could still reach out and snatch him back. It was not until 1951, when we were given the chance at new lives in a wonderful new country, the United States of America, that he was finally able to relax and live out his life in grateful peace.

Over the years, I often wondered about the voice I heard on that fall day in 1947. Could the voice have belonged to some kind neighbor who had guessed my destination and decided to warn me anonymously? Or perhaps it really was the voice of God that prompted me to turn around. But whether the voice was human or heavenly, of this I am certain: God answered the prayer of my heart, and it was His hand that guided us safely back together so we could be a family again.

Time and time again the Lord has been petitioned for many requests. Many are simple matters and easily taken care of. But Bob's request was by no means simple and by no means easily taken care of. But with God, all things are possible.

Miracle Behind the Iron Curtain

BY BOB KELLY, SUN LAKES, ARIZONA

It was 3:00 A.M. on June 25, 1977. I was kneeling by my bed in a hotel room in Oradea, Romania, hundreds of miles behind the Iron Curtain. An hour before, I had been arrested by the Communist police, who earlier that night had taken my partner, Sven, into custody for the "crime" of carrying a suitcase filled with Bibles.

We worked for an international ministry dedicated to taking Bibles and other Christian materials into Iron Curtain countries. Sven was an experienced courier, but this was my first trip. I was a very young Christian, only two years old in Christ, and I was terrified. Our van, filled with approximately 1500 New Testaments and songbooks concealed from general view, had been seized, and I had visions of Communist agents searching it and finding our precious cargo.

We were told to report back to police headquarters at eight o'clock in the morning. With our secret exposed, I fully expected to be sentenced to a long prison term, as other Bible "smugglers" had been. As I knelt, close to despair, I thought of my family, thousands of miles away, and the circumstances that had led me in two short years from the presidency of a Florida bank to this place, where I had no one to turn to for help—no one, that is, except the all-powerful God I had recently come to know.

I took out the small Bible I had brought with me, which somehow had escaped detection by my Communist captors. Turning to Acts

16, I read the story of the miraculous release of Paul and Silas from prison. Trapped as we were, hundreds of miles behind the Iron Curtain, our predicament was almost as precarious.

Nevertheless, I prayed this seemingly impossible prayer: "Lord, I know You're the same today as You were 2000 years ago, with the same miraculous powers. Open our prison doors, I pray, and restore us to freedom within 24 hours."

My partner and I endured three hours of questioning the next morning. Then, to our amazement, we were told we could leave. Our passports and the keys to our van were exactly as we had left them. The secret compartments holding our "contraband" were intact.

However, we were by no means out of danger, as three Communist borders and hundreds of miles lay between us and freedom. The Romanian police followed us all the way to the border, where the guards merely waved us through the barriers. The Yugoslav guards did the same as we entered their country. Again, we were closely followed.

When we got close to the Yugoslav/Austrian border, Sven told me to stop. "We're not allowed to cross at night," he explained, "because traffic is light and the guards pass their time by carefully searching the few vehicles that arrive."

I persuaded him to get close enough for us to at least check out the situation. To our surprise and delight, the line of cars approaching from the Austrian side was extremely heavy. With barely a glance, the busy Yugoslav guards waved us on our way.

As we entered Austria, I looked at my watch. It was 3:00 A.M. Exactly 24 hours had passed since I had prayed that seemingly impossible prayer. We were free. We were safe. And I was praising God for His miraculous provision.

Many times the Lord places the need in our hearts to do something very special. We know we are meant to do this one thing, but do not have the resources. Sharon and Ted prayed for God to provide the means. It did not take long for them to watch the miracle unfold.

Missionary Miracle

BY SHARON HINCK, BLOOMINGTON, MINNESOTA

The paper vibrated in my quivering hands, as if it, too, could feel my excitement. Delight surged through my heart as I read the letter a second time.

Dear Sharon:

We invite you to come and train our outreach team again this January, and we'd love you to stay longer than two weeks this time. I know it's hard to leave your family, so we'd like to extend an invitation to bring them along. Your husband, Ted, could help with the promotional video we plan to produce, while you teach the classes. Would it be possible to stay for a full month? I'll arrange someone on the mission base to watch your kids during the day. Let me know if this works for you and your family. We all miss you.

In Him,

Kenny

Kenny led an evangelistic team for Youth With A Mission. The group, Windows, gathered young people from around the world, formed teams, and trained them at their base in Hong Kong. In addition to Bible study, they learned mime and dance as forms of evangelism. The team then traveled all year to locations as diverse as professional ballet schools in Japan, remote villages in Africa, or nightclubs in Amsterdam. They shared the gospel in a universal language that breaks down all barriers. My time with Windows had been the highlight of my career as a choreographer and ballet teacher.

"Ted, Ted!" I flapped my arms wildly, running toward the basement.

My husband tromped up the stairs from the basement. "What's the matter?"

The twinkle I loved in my husband's eyes had been fading as of late. The video company he worked for had not been able to meet payroll for weeks. He could not afford to keep working without a salary, but his job search had brought nothing but discouragement.

"It all makes sense now!" I pulled him into the kitchen and danced a quick jig around him. "I know why God hasn't answered our prayers for you for a new job." I waved the letter under his nose.

Ted snatched the letter from my hand. I bit my lip and watched him read.

A spark ignited in his eyes. "Hmmm, maybe. We've never had a time we could just pull up and leave for a month until now." He ran a hand through his blond curls.

"Isn't it wonderful?" I jumped into his arms. "I bet this is what God was planning all along."

"Aren't Joel and Katie a little young to be missionaries though, Sharon?"

I grinned. At ages six and four, they would be an entertaining addition to the base. "They're the perfect age to be missionaries."

Ted laughed and spun me around. I threw back my head, watching the kitchen spiral past, and my head never stopped spinning during the coming days.

First things first. Ted and I went to speak with our pastor.

"We don't have any savings, and the practical thing to do would be to hunker down and keep searching for a job. But it feels like God is tugging at us to do this. What do you think? Are we being saintly or stupid?" My husband leaned close to make sure he gleaned whatever wisdom our pastor might have to pass on.

Pastor Tim shrugged. "Maybe both." He leaned forward and smiled. "And that's all right."

I flipped open the notebook where I had brainstormed the pros and cons. "We have to come up with 2500 dollars for the plane fare, but they'll house and feed us at the base in Hong Kong."

Our pastor stroked his beard, "Well, I know you want God's guidance, and this could very well be His way of giving it to you. If He wants you to go, you know just as well as I do, He's more than capable of providing the funds."

That night after supper, we explained the plan to Joel and Katie.

"Kids, this is our donation box. We're going to leave it here, right on the table. If God fills it by the time we're supposed to get our airplane tickets, then we'll go to Hong Kong." I watched the children for their reaction after my husband explained the situation to them.

Joel tore from the table and raced upstairs to his attic bedroom. I thought he was devastated at the idea of leaving, but he bounded back to the kitchen a minute later with a fist full of allowance money. "Here." He dropped one dollar and 73 cents into the mission box as our first donation.

We sent out letters, spoke to the Bible class at church, and baked hundreds of gingerbread men to give out during fellowship hour, requesting just a small donation. Every day, we continued to pray.

Our church's missionary board was eager to help, but could only give 50 dollars at the most from their small fund.

Little by little, the box on our table began to fill. Ted continued hunting for a job, but without success. We felt that was just another confirmation that God was keeping us free for the work He wanted done in Hong Kong.

But we had another worry. We could not afford to pay the mortgage on our house while it stood empty for a month. And who would want to rent it for a short four weeks? Through the grapevine, we learned of a couple returning on sabbatical from mission work in Japan. They needed a place to stay for exactly one month—the same month we would be in Hong Kong.

Everything was falling into place, until the day we had to turn in the money for our airline tickets. Ted and I sat at the kitchen table and emptied the box of donations. We were 500 dollars short. Ted stared at the calculator and added the amount again, hoping it would change.

The phone rang, breaking our sullen silence. I reached for the phone. "Hello?"

"Hi, Sharon. It's Gordon. Can Ted stop by the church to pick up the mission-board check? We have it ready for you and haven't had a chance to drop it by."

I hid my discouragement and promised to pass along the message. Fifty dollars would not go very far toward our needed 500 dollars.

Ted took Joel and Katie with him to collect the check from the mission board, and quiet overtook my home. I sank deep in my chair and lowered my forehead to the surface of the kitchen table. "God, I thought I had it all figured out. This is so hard. Is it our own fault? Do we have enough faith? Did we miss Your will?"

Even as I whispered the words, I heard our pastor's last sermon in my mind: "It's not about our efforts. It's about God's effort on our behalf. He loves you. You don't have to earn that."

"Lord, thank You for loving us. But it's not looking good for us to go to Hong Kong, and it's certainly not looking good staying here, either. No job, no mission trip, no answers. Help me trust You, Father."

Tears glittered on the tabletop as I continued praying. After a while I felt the burden ease. And then I heard Ted walk through the door with the children. He walked with calculated steps, almost like he moved toward the altar on our wedding day.

Without a word, he handed me the check from the mission board. I blinked three times, and the extra zero still remained. I thought it was a by-product of my tear-weary eyes. But I looked again. Sure enough, it was a check for 500 dollars—the exact amount we needed, and only a few hours before the travel agent's office closed.

Ted grinned. "I guess God wants us in Hong Kong."

Our time with Windows was wonderful. We supported their team, shared our faith, and grew in our own convictions as well.

After we returned home, I expected God to reward us with a great new job for Ted. I sent out a report about our trip to all of our supporters, and then sat back and waited for Ted's new job to materialize. But our faith was stretched further as I realized that God does not follow my script, nor does He return one favor for another. After a series of odd jobs, Ted did eventually find work with another video company.

Our children will always remember the box on the table, our answered prayers, and the miracle mission trip. And Ted and I will remember that God provides. When He wants something done, He does it His way. A life of prayer can be challenging, and God does not always work the way we expect Him to, but His love carries His purpose through, without a doubt.

In our country of wealth and prosperity, many items are taken for granted. Many of the needs for which our Lord provides come to us without struggle or strife. Susy learned that for one man, in a country far from here, prayer was the only way.

Drive-by Blessing

BY SUSANNA FLORY, CASTRO VALLEY, CALIFORNIA

Cuba is such a hot and sweaty place, but the people there always look unwrinkled, unhurried, and spotless. I do not know how they do it. Many Cubans own only one shirt—a shirt without wrinkles and stains. On the other hand, my traveling companions and I were rumpled, cranky, and sticky.

Toward the end of our nine-day mission trip to Cuba, we decided to make one final stop that we called a "drive-by blessing." God led us to a small house church in the town of Candelaria. When we knocked on the door of the small, dusty building, we interrupted a meeting of five Cuban missionaries, all in their twenties. Later, we found out they were in the midst of fasting and praying for help.

They greeted each of us, nine in all, with kisses on the cheek and murmurs of "Gloria de Dios." We joined our brothers on rickety wooden benches and communicated with the little bit of Spanish we knew. They did not seem to be surprised to see us at all and treated us as honored guests, fully expected.

One by one, the Cuban missionaries shared their stories. One of them had been a priest of Santeria. His face, alive with the light of the Lord, belied the scar on his hand—a relic of his blood initiation into the voodoo-like cult.

Another man had been a street fighter, the evidence of his former life in his bulging muscles. "If it weren't for Jesus, I'd be dead, in prison, or insane," he told us.

Then there was Sandi. He had short brown hair, a close-trimmed mustache, and gentle, chocolate-colored eyes. His white pants and gray polo shirt were clean and looked like they had just been ironed. What I did not notice was that the seat of his pants was ripped wide open.

Sandi was a pastor's son, but had been rebellious. When his father started a house church in their home, he ran out the back door whenever it was time for a service and carried on wildly in town. One day, while he was on the run, he broke down and prayed for God's direction. Shortly after that, he found the Candelaria house church, where he surrendered his heart to the Lord. Today he was visiting the pastor who had mentored him for two years.

While Sandi spoke, I heard a creaking noise from the back of the church. Doug, one of the men from our team, was headed outside.

Doug was a man who loved people. While the rest of us fretted about meetings, bagging medical supplies, or prepping for puppet shows, Doug would be off playing catch with the neighborhood kids, waving out the window of our van, or gleefully trying out his mangled Spanish on pastors and church workers.

Doug was very perceptive and noticed things we did not. He saw kids who needed a friend, and hurting people in need of a kind word. He had also seen and taken note of the rip in Sandi's pants.

Within a few minutes, Doug headed back into the church with a nice pair of pants, Levi Dockers, fished from his suitcase. While another Cuban missionary spoke, Doug walked to the back of the church with Sandi, spoke a few words in his trademark Spanglish, and handed him the pair of pants with a quick hug. I didn't think that much about it, as we had handed out all kinds of personal items.

Soon is was time to be leaving, so we dug deep into our fanny packs to give them some much-needed funds. As we said our goodbyes, Sandi stepped forward. "Wait. I have something to tell you." His voice was trembling a bit.

"Yesterday I rode the bus for five hours to come to Candelaria to pray with my friends," Sandi said, looking around at the other four men. "When I climbed up the steps of the bus, the back of my pants ripped open. They are the only pair I have."

He turned to Doug, his eyes moist with tears. "I just want to let you know that God answers prayer." His faith hit me hard. It was like a physical presence in the room, alive.

I thought of something I had heard from a friend long ago: "It's an upside-down world with the Lord." When I asked her what she meant, she said, "The Cubans are rich and we are poor. They live on faith; we live on MasterCard."

Doug walked toward Sandi, weeping, and put his arm around his shoulders. The rest of us were silent, amazed, and broken.

Sandi continued with a simple statement that cut us to the heart. He proudly held up his new pair of pants and said, "God provides everything we need."

We can pray for a good day, good health, and good friends. We can pray for many small things that always seem to come true. But when it comes to really big, important prayers, do we truly believe God can answer them? Jim Brock will never again doubt what prayer can do.

Simple Faith

BY MURIEL LARSON, GREENVILLE, SOUTH CAROLINA

Missionary Jim Brock traveled past the thirsty fields of corn, grain, and peanuts. He sighed for the people of Benin. The sun scorched the ground, beating down on the young crops. Benin had not seen rain in five or six weeks, and if it didn't rain soon, the new plants would die. Even if the farmers had any extra seed left and replanted, the harvest would be sparse.

Jim had been serving in Benin for many years and had started a number of churches in this small republic of West Africa. As soon as he reached his home, he began to pray earnestly for rain, just as the churches were.

One day Baco, one of the pastors who ministered to a congregation seven miles away, rode to the mission station on his bicycle. "Pastor," he said, "I want you to come with me to our village to join the men in our church to pray for rain."

Jim put Baco's bike in the back of his jeep, and the two men took off for Kouberi. When they arrived, they saw crowds of people gathered. Witch doctors were jumping around, cutting themselves, and shouting to their gods. One was making a sacrifice. All of those around them were shouting and crying aloud.

"What's going on here, Baco?" Jim could not believe his eyes.

"For the past seven days, they have been praying to their god to send rain," Baco explained. "Today the village chief came to see me, asking if we Christians would pray also. Of course, we have been praying, but now the chief has officially put us to the public task of praying. That's why I came to get you."

We rounded up 16 Christian men and gathered them in the church to pray for rain. "Pastor, can you stay here until the rains begin?"

This may take days. There's no sign of rain, Father. And I never told my wife, Sandy, where I was going. She'll be worried.

Baco noticed the hesitation and the look on Jim's face. "Pastor, you have taught us that everything God wrote in His Word is true, and you've taught us that God would answer our prayers. So if we pray for this rain, by His promise and His Word, He will do it, for our need is great."

"I will stay."

The men decided that Jim would begin their prayer, and each man would pray in turn. They would not stop until rain came. The 18 men prayed in turn, and then again. People gathered around the church, peering into the windows. Jim got up and closed the shutters. They continued around the circle again.

Suddenly the men heard the window shutters banging against the walls. Usually, in Benin, strong winds precede rain.

They continued praying, and Jim asked the Lord to forgive his doubt and unbelief. All of a sudden, the wind tore one end of the church roof off and, with a mighty roar, the men began praying simultaneously. Jim pleaded with the Lord to forgive his unbelief again, and the wind began to die down.

Then Jim heard the sweet sound of great raindrops pelting on what was left of the metal roof of the church. Faster and louder, the rain poured down a cacophony of sound to greet the ears of these faithful men. They leapt to their feet and ran outside, shouting for joy and praising God for bringing the much-needed rain. The village people joined them.

Many people came to thank Jim, Baco, and the other Christian men for praying. The chief also came to them. "Your God is more powerful than ours. From now on, every year when the crops are planted, we will call on you Christians to pray for the rain."

For three days the rain poured down, and the crops were saved. Jim knew the impact that saving the crops had on the people of Benin and continually reminds other people of his experience.

"This experience made me realize that it's not enough for us to just study God's Word and teach that it is true. Too often we tend to get in a rut and forget that it really is Truth. When faced with a test or trial, we tend to rationalize, as I had done." Jim then reminded himself, "That day, through a man I had trained in Bible school, God reminded me that His promises not only apply to biblical days, but they apply even now, to every area of our lives."

10
The Prayers God Always Says Yes To

We all like to get a resounding yes to our prayers. And in some ways, every prayer *is* answered yes if we believe by faith that God causes all things to work together for our good, as we read in Romans 8:28. But to be truthful, when a loved one we have prayed for dies or a job we desperately wanted goes to someone else, or the money we think we need does not arrive on our timetable, sometimes God's answer seems like a very certain no.

There are some prayers, however, that never get a no from God. The first of these prayers is the prayer that asks God to change our life from where we *were* going to where God wants us to go. It is the prayer that brings us into the family of God with the assurance of an eternity in heaven after we leave this earth.

In my previous anthologies, *God Allows U-Turns,* I have chronicled many such stories as people from every conceivable background let down their defenses and surrendered their lives to Christ.

The other kind of prayer God always says yes to is the prayer that asks God to use us to touch the lives of other people. It is the prayer that simply says, "Here am I, God. Send me." It has often been said that the only ability God really requires of us is *avail-ability.*

This final chapter offers a few such stories wherein God answered these two kinds of prayers. My prayer is that you, too, may experience both of these kinds of yes prayers.

Your word, O Lord, is eternal; it stands firm in the heavens. Your faithfulness continues through all generations (Psalm 119:89-90).

Have you ever felt the life you dreamed of and deserved was unjustly snatched from your grasp? Have you felt devastated because your dreams never came true? Perhaps all you needed was to pray for help to find your way, just as John learned to do.

The Day the Cheering Stopped

BY GLORIA CASSITY STARGEL, GAINSVILLE, GEORGIA
(AS TOLD BY JOHN C. STEWART)

It happened on a cold day in January, midway through my senior year in high school. I tossed my books into the locker and reached for my black-and-gold Cougar jacket. From down the corridor, a friend called out, "Good luck, Johnny. I hope you get the school you want."

Playing football was more than a game for me. It was my *life*. So the world looked pretty wonderful as I headed up the hill toward the gym to learn which college wanted me on its team.

How I counted on the resulting scholarship. I had for years! It held my only hope for higher education. My dad, an alcoholic, had left home long ago, and Mom worked two jobs just to keep seven children fed. I held down part-time jobs to help out.

I wasn't worried; I had the grades I needed. Ever since grammar school, I had lived and breathed football. It was my identity. Growing up in a little southern town where football is king, my skills on the field made me a big man in the community, as well as on campus. I pictured myself right up there on that pedestal.

And everyone around me pumped that ego. The local newspaper mentioned me in write-ups. At football games, exuberant cheerleaders yelled out my name. People said things like, "You can do it, Johnny.

You can go all the way to professional football!" I mean, that was heady stuff, and I ate it up. It kind of made up for my not having a dad to encourage me along the way.

Hurrying to the gym that day, I recalled all those football games—and all those *injuries!* I never had let any of them slow me down for long—not the broken back, nor the messed-up shoulders and knees. I just gritted my teeth and played right through the agony. I *had* to.

Now came the reward. A good future would be worth the price I had paid. So with a confident grin on my face, I sprinted into Coach Stone's office.

Coach sat behind his desk, the papers from my file spread before him. Our three other coaches sat around the room. No doubt about it—this lineup signaled a momentous occasion.

"Have a seat, Johnny." Coach motioned to the chair beside his desk. "Johnny," he started, "you've worked really hard. You've done a good job for us. Several colleges want to make you an offer."

Something about his tone made me nervous. I shifted my sitting position.

"But, Johnny," he said, holding my medical records in his hands, "Doctor Kendley can't recommend you for college football. One more bad hit, and you could be paralyzed for life. We can't risk it."

A long silence followed. Then Coach Stone's eyes met mine. "I'm sorry, Johnny. There will be no scholarship."

No scholarship? The blow hit me like a 300-pound linebacker slamming against my chest. Somehow I got out of that office. I could not understand that they were simply thinking of my welfare. Instead, in my mind a punching bag reverberated, *You're not good enough. You're not good enough. You're not good enough.*

For me the cheering stopped. Without the cheering, I was nothing. And without college, I would *stay* a nothing.

After that, I just gave up. In so doing, I lost my moorings. At first, I settled for beer and marijuana. Soon I got into the hard stuff:

acid, PCP, heroin, cocaine—I tried them all. When graduation rolled around, I wonder how I even made it through the ceremonies.

Several older friends tried to talk to me about God. Yet even though I had grown up in church, had even served as an altar boy, I could not grasp the fact that God had anything to do with my present problems.

I decided to hit the road with a couple of buddies. We had no money and no goal. Along the way, we got into stealing gas to keep us going. When we got hungry enough, we picked up some odd jobs. No matter how little food we had, we always managed somehow to get more drugs.

My anger continued to fester. It wasn't long until I got into a bad fight and landed in jail thousands of miles from home. It caused me to take a good look at myself and see how low I had sunk. This began my slow U-turn back to God.

"God," I prayed for the first time in years, "please help me. I'm lost and I can't find my way back."

I didn't hear an immediate answer, nor did I clean up my act. We *did* head toward home, but the old car had enjoyed enough. It quit.

I went into a garage, hoping to get some cheap parts. Maybe I could patch her up enough to get us home. I was tired, hungry, dirty, and very much under the influence. Yet a man there extended a hand of friendship. He even took us to supper.

After we were fed, Mr. Brown called me aside. "Son," he said, "you don't have to live like this. You can be somebody if only you'll try. God will help you. Remember, He loves you, and so do I."

I was buffaloed. He seemed really to care about me and called me "son." It had been a long, long time since a man had called me "son."

That night in my sleeping bag, I gazed up at the star-filled Texas night. The sky looked so close, I thought maybe I could reach up and touch it. Once again, I tried to pray. "Lord, I am *so* tired. If You'll have me, I'm ready to come back to You."

In my heart, I heard Him answer, "I'm here. Come on back, son. I'm here." He called me "son," just like Mr. Brown did! I liked that.

On the road again, I started thinking that if Mr. Brown, a complete stranger, thought I could make something of myself, maybe I could.

I didn't straighten out all at once. But I started trying, and God kept sending people to help me, like Susan. In September this cute, young thing—a casual friend from high school—came up to me at a football game, of all places. She kissed me on the cheek. "Welcome home, Johnny." The day she told me, "Johnny, if you keep doing drugs, I can't date you anymore," is the day I quit them for good.

Susan and I married, and today have three beautiful children. We are active in our local church and operate a successful business. I can tell you it means the world to me having earned the respect of my community.

All these years later, I still can feel the sting of that day—the day the cheering stopped. The hurt does not linger, though. Once my U-turn was complete, I learned I could live without the cheers. After all, I have a caring heavenly Father who calls me "son."

Which reminds me, I *do* have a cheering section—a heavenly one. Check out this Bible verse I discovered: "There is rejoicing in the presence of the angels of God over one sinner who repents" (Luke 15:10).

How about that? Angels! Cheering for *me!* I like that.

Have you ever faced a situation where you knew you needed to pray, but you did not know how to pray? The situation seemed beyond you, perhaps beyond God. And yet somehow you knew that prayer was the key, and that you *must* pray the problem through to its solution. Phyllis Wallace's wonderful story reminds us that though we may not know the answer, God certainly does. We can always go to Him with nothing more than an urgent, "Help, God!"

Get on Your Knees When You Don't Know What to Do

BY PHYLLIS WALLACE, COLLINSVILLE, ILLINOIS

The retreat center was unfamiliar. I was with people I barely knew, from a church persuasion other than mine. It was an uncomfortable feeling. I had been swept up in the enthusiasm of a friend who said I had not lived until I went to a women's retreat.

Everybody else obviously enjoyed being there. They exchanged stories and recipes. They did not seem at all worried that their husbands would wash the rugs and the bras in the same load of laundry while they were gone! This was living?

The social hour segued into devotion time. Our guest speaker lived up to her first name, "Win." Her winsomeness pulled me into the topic from the very first word. I do not remember the topic now, but I do remember my soul being fed as she quoted Scripture. It related to the chaos going on in my life. My mom and dad loved and served Jesus Christ. They taught me to do the same. I worshiped regularly, studied my Bible, and loved Christ, but this unexpected "feeding" was supplemental, savory, and sweet.

The uniqueness was in Win's openness and vulnerability. She shared the struggles and victories of her Christian walk and was not embarrassed about what had not worked. She had asked for forgiveness and turned it over to God. She was humble, not arrogant about her successes. The tender compassion she felt for the things of God reached into my heart and made me want to share something I had not been able to tell anyone. I had a burning question about a dilemma I faced and could not conquer. Maybe she was smart enough to know the answer, but how would I approach her? Would anyone else find out? Did she keep confidences? She was from another state. We would never see each other again, so I decided to give it a try.

The first evening, I waited my turn to talk with Win, stammering out that I would like to talk to her alone. She graciously offered her room and made an appointment to meet there later. As I poured out my troubled story, I watched her reaction. She listened carefully, nodded, and made an occasional comment. I was just sure she understood my dilemma and would know exactly what I should do to remedy my endlessly conflicted situation.

Then came a surprise. We sat on single beds across from one another in the sparse room. Win looked deeply into my eyes and said frankly, "I don't know what to tell you. I have no idea what you must do, but God does. Let's talk to Him about it."

Then she got down on her knees, on that cold, bare floor. So did I. Kneeling together, she led the entire prayer, skillfully and succinctly committing all we had discussed into God's hands. With a confident "Amen!" she finished praying and cheerfully told me to keep in touch.

I left behind some of the load I had carried for years. I discovered that it did not matter that she had not given me a "to-do" list to remedy my situation. Previously I had prayed incessantly about the situation, but this time it was different. I picked up on Win's confidence in Christ. It made such a difference that I still reflect on it to this day. God's Spirit met me in that room through the prayer of a woman who totally trusted Him for every detail of her life and for every detail of mine.

Twenty years later, the spin-off of that kneeling moment, woman to woman to God, continues to impact my life. Did the situation we lifted up to the Lord go away? No. Something else did. My fear and doubt that God was in control evaporated. Jesus beckoned with outstretched arms: "Come to Me. I am your shield." He says it to all of us in His Word, which I read with more understanding now as I yield to His power and peace.

Now I copy Win's model of going to my knees in prayer. Literally all around the world, God has sent women into my life who needed to kneel before Him. I have been privileged to kneel beside them. I do not have to worry about knowing the answer to their dilemma. *God* knows.

When we pray to help other people find the Lord and understand Him like we do, we often discover many things. Sometimes it is not what we say, but what we do that really matters.

A Nurse's Prayer

BY PENELOPE CARLEVATO, KNOXVILLE, TENNESSEE

As I walked across the parking lot into the hospital that hot, August afternoon, I prayed that God would use me to bring His love to my patients. As a registered nurse, I had many opportunities to pray for patients and their families and to be a vessel for God's use.

My heart was hurting this particular day for one of my patients: a young man with a precious wife and a dear little towheaded, two-year-old son.

Donald (not his real name) had been diagnosed with leukemia about a year ago, and the nursing staff had witnessed his body's gradual decline. Now he was in his last days, and his beautiful young wife remained by his bedside. She would slip out of his room frequently, lean against the wall, and weep. If their little two-year-old was there, he would wrap his chubby arms around her legs and ask, "'Mommy, why are you sad?"

When Donald was first admitted to the hospital, he had been pleasant and friendly, but with each successive admission for chemotherapy, he became more angry and withdrawn. Each visit kept him longer and longer, and whenever he was my patient, I prayed, "God, give me the right words to say, and help him to be open to hearing about You." He always remained polite but curt, and left very little opportunity for me to share with him.

That morning at church, the guest speaker had shared from Matthew 25:42-44 and talked about how when we minister to other people, we also minister to Jesus. I could understand the idea of blessing other people with Jesus, but was not too clear about ministering *to* Him. So I prayed that morning for God to show me how to minister to and bless Him. But that was the farthest thing from my mind as I arrived at work.

That evening after arriving, I started going from room to room, getting my assigned patients ready for the night. I came to Donald's room, and as I entered his doorway, I prayed, "Please, God, open Donald's heart and let me minister to him." I felt this could be my last chance. He was now only skin and bones, and every vertebra and joint showed through his transparent skin. He always sat up because it was impossible for him to breathe if he lay down. He leaned forward over a padded T-shaped frame that a friend had made for him. The room was dim and quiet, except for his labored breathing. I gave him his medications, hung a new IV bottle, and straightened his bed.

"Donald," I quietly said, "what can I do to make you more comfortable?"

He replied in a soft, raspy whisper, more like a man of advanced years than a man in his late twenties: "Please, could you rub my back? It hurts so much."

As I carefully rubbed lotion on his back, I began to pray for him, and again prayed for the right words. Nothing. I closed my eyes and focused on Jesus as I kept massaging his fragile back. Donald seemed to be relaxing a little, his breathing quieter and slower. A feeling of peacefulness invaded the room. I opened my eyes, and instead of Donald in the bed, there sat Jesus. I closed my eyes quickly. I must be mistaken. I peeked again. Again I saw Jesus. I kept rubbing the back of Jesus, and a feeling of perfect peace invaded the room. Then very slowly, Donald appeared back in his bed.

By now he had fallen asleep, and I quietly left the room.

Oh, thank You, Jesus. I don't know how it happened that I saw You. I just know I did.

I had said more to Donald by my actions than by words—a valuable lesson for someone frequently concerned with "saying the right thing." I realized in that moment that when we are available and willing to serve other people, we are truly ministering to Jesus.

At one time or another, you or someone you know has prayed
to the Lord to help save a loved one and bring him to the Lord.
We can never be sure when or where the event will take place.
We need only have the faith that it will. John's family would
never have expected an icy road to be a part of it.

Meeting in a Snowbank

BY DR. TOM C. RAKOW, SILVER LAKE, MINNESOTA

The phone call came one cold, wintry afternoon. One of the members of my congregation had been admitted to the hospital for emergency surgery. Snow flurries and icy roads made for a tense trip to the hospital. I had been feeling discouraged, and my discouragement added to the day's dreariness.

I arrived at the hospital and read a portion of Scripture and prayed with my parishioner before he was taken to surgery. Knowing that it would be hours before he awoke, I headed home.

A few miles from the hospital, I saw a car in a snowbank. A man was sitting on the passenger side with the vehicle's engine running. The cold weather caused me to think of my dad who has breathing problems. I pulled my car over to the side of the road, even though everything appeared to be under control, and walked up to the stuck car.

When the man lowered his window, I asked, "Is everything all right?"

He answered me in short breaths, with a raspy voice: "My wife... was bringing me back from the hospital...and hit a slick spot. Someone stopped...and she...went with them to get a tow truck."

I said, "Okay," and turned to leave. Suddenly I found myself asking this stranger, "Do you mind if I wait with you until the tow truck comes?" I must have appeared to pose no threat, as he consented.

As I slid in behind the steering wheel, I heard a religious program playing softly on the car radio. The man, whose name was John, explained that he had cancer in his chest. I immediately knew John and I were not sitting together in the car by mere coincidence. I knew that, at that moment, both of us were exactly where God wanted us.

A question surfaced in my mind. At first I tried to suppress it. But then, sensing a great urgency, I asked, "John, have you accepted Jesus Christ as your Savior and Lord?"

John looked me straight in the eyes. With great difficulty, he said, "I've been trying to find God, but I don't know how."

I explained to John how he could receive Jesus Christ as his Savior and Lord. I read from the Gospel of John, where Jesus promised, "I tell you the truth, whoever hears my word and believes him who sent me has eternal life and will not be condemned; he has crossed over from death to life" (John 5:24). John prayed, asking Jesus to forgive him for his sins and to come into his life.

After the tow truck arrived, I wrote down some Bible verses for John to look up when he got home. As I handed John the paper, he grabbed my hand and said, "Thank you for stopping. I've been waiting for you....for a long time!"

John died a month later. Although a virtual stranger, I was asked to participate in John's funeral. A relative told me John lost his voice shortly after I met him. They had not known John had been saved that night, but they did know he had experienced great peace before he passed away.

I told them about our meeting that night. They were overjoyed to hear that their prayers for John's salvation had been answered. Many of John's friends and family had been praying a very long time for John to receive Christ.

I truly marvel at how God uses events to create just the right situation to orchestrate His plans for us. He put me in the right place at the right time to answer the prayers of John's loved ones and bring John to salvation, before it was too late.

> The power of prayer is a proven fact. Sandra knows that. For one day, in a crowd of over 100,000 people, God found two people to reunite, all due to one prayer.

Answered Prayer-on-a-Stick

BY SANDRA SNIDER, ST. ANTHONY, MINNESOTA

The Minnesota State Fair is also known as the "Great Minnesota Get-Together." It is a 12-day annual extravaganza that is synonymous with Pronto Pups, cheese curds, deep-fried candy bars, and buckets of french fries. As an eight-year employee of the annual end-of-summer rite, I was working for the transportation department. My job as a courtesy driver included shuttling all kinds of people—food demonstrators, musicians, cattle judges, swine judges, and dairy princesses—in a golf cart. I also shuttled plenty of lost people, too. Fair-goers can easily become separated from family and friends in the large crowd. This is an event that attracts more than 1.7 million guests each year.

It was in this 25-different-foods-on-a-stick setting where I encountered the power of prayer. A friend told me she asks God to bring people into her life who need prayer. During my shift at the fairgrounds one day, I decided to pray for that same opportunity. I told God that I was willing to be used as a vessel in any way He desired. "Send someone to me who needs a touch from You," I prayed.

The person God chose to send my way was Ann, a somewhat rude and irritating elderly woman who had become separated from her 32-year-old daughter. Ann was upset, distraught, and worried sick. The way she carried on, though, you would think her daughter was 2 instead of 32. I reminded her that her daughter was a mature woman. "What does it matter how old she is!" she barked at me.

I was told to transport Ann to her parked car. Perhaps the daughter was waiting there or had at least left a note as to her whereabouts on the windshield. As soon as Ann climbed into the seat next to me, I began to sense the Lord wanted me to pray out loud for this lost soul and the predicament she found herself in. "Not this woman, Lord," I argued silently. "She's irritating me." I was not exactly enamored with the woman God had sent my way. I brushed off the Master and maneuvered my golf cart through the swarming crowds.

We located Ann's car. There was no sign of her daughter and no note. *I might as well return this woman to Care and Assistance and let them deal with her,* I thought. But the Lord's insistence to pray continued, and my spirit finally relented when the pressure became too intense.

I asked Ann if it was all right if I prayed. "I suppose so," was her flat, disinterested response. I pulled the golf cart over to a more secluded place and turned the engine off. I then began to pray out loud. "Father God, You tell us that we have no wisdom apart from You. We need Your wisdom today. You tell us that if we ask for Your wisdom, You will give it to us abundantly and continuously. We need Your help in reuniting Ann with her daughter. You tell us that not a sparrow falls to the ground without You knowing it. You are aware of this situation. Help Ann take hold of faith and not fear. I am confident that You will work this out because You are able. Amen!"

Ann fidgeted while I prayed. *Well, a lot of good this did,* I thought. *Why couldn't God send me someone who is more agreeable to pray with?*

I returned Ann to Care and Assistance and suggested she wait there. They would try to assist her. She bolted out the door. I had no choice but to follow her, and as I did, I was surprised to hear Ann shouting her daughter's name. The high level of relief at spotting her daughter caused Ann to fling her purse and belongings to the ground and run after her daughter. Nothing was going to encumber or delay this reunion! When Ann finally caught up with her daughter, she put her face in her hands and sobbed. Then came an exclamation that took me back a few steps: "She prayed! She prayed!"

The realization of what had happened hit me when the two women disappeared into the crowd, arm in arm. I sat glued to the idle golf cart, oblivious to the pressing crowds around me. Tears came to my eyes. I spiritually and emotionally processed the powerful way in which God had just answered my prayer.

Less than five minutes after I finished praying with Ann, the two women were hugging necks. They had been separated for more than four hours. The fair attendance was 111,000 that day. What were the chances of Ann bumping into her daughter at the exact moment she ran out of Care and Assistance? What were the chances of a lost mother connecting with her daughter among 4.3 million square feet of exhibit space on 320 acres of land? I wondered how this experience would touch Ann's heart. Would it give her increased faith in a God who indeed cared?

Without paying the seven-dollar admission fee, God made an appearance at the Minnesota State Fair and answered my prayer. His was the grandstand show to end all grandstand shows!

The opportunity to witness occurs every day, most times in a situation we have prepared for and are aware of. Although Richard had prayed for the Lord to use him as a witness, he did not realize the Lord would answer quite so quickly.

No Small Miracle

BY R. T. BYRUM, MARRIETA, GEORGIA

"Lord, please use me as a witness to spread the Good News, not by preaching on a street corner, but by serving others by example. God, You open the doors of opportunity to witness for You. Help me to see it when You present it. Thank You so much," I prayed fervently with the rest of the congregation.

My family was attending a worldwide conference for our denomination in Pensacola, Florida. The sermons we heard inspired not only me, but my wife and our school-aged sons. Each of us wanted to be the witness God desired us to be.

I tried to be an example in my workplace by keeping a Bible prominently displayed on my desk. If a client or vendor asked if I studied the Scriptures, I would nod and smile. Sometimes they would ask a simple question that could be answered quickly, but other times a discussion might extend through lunch. It was not much, but in my world of existence, it was my only point of contact with other people outside my church.

The conference finished with a final admonition of witnessing to other people, and my family and I returned to our rooms for the last time before checkout. We decided to use our extra time after packing, enjoying some last-minute relaxation. My sons decided to swim with friends they had met, and my wife was browsing the hotel gift shop. As for me, I was relaxing on our ground-floor patio, enjoying a novel.

I don't know why I glanced up from my book, but as I did, I noticed a barefoot girl, possibly in her late twenties. She was dressed in blue jeans and a long-sleeved flannel shirt to protect against the stiff morning breeze. Wind-tossed sand danced around her, and she turned this way and that to avoid the stinging grains.

Her dark, shoulder-length hair, soaked with sea spray, hung limply around her face. She seemed to be carrying a heavy burden. Her shoulders were sagging, and every so often she would bend down and sift her fingers through the sand before moving on.

She made her way closer to my patio and not only did I hear the sounds of the shore, but the unexpected sound of sobbing filled my ears. I had just reached a pivotal point in my Clive Cussler novel, but the urgency to make sure the young girl was okay lifted me out of my chair and out of my comfort zone. The sky was looming with storm clouds, and I was tempted to turn around and make my way back to my room. But the urgency only strengthened.

She didn't notice me until I touched her arm. Startled, she quickly dabbed at her eyes with her shirtsleeve. I introduced myself and asked if she needed assistance.

"No, thank you. I...I lost my keys is all."

I nodded my head in understanding. "Your room keys, huh?"

She sighed and wiped her eyes again. "No, I could deal with losing them. I've lost my car keys, and I'm supposed to be on the road back to Georgia to meet my grandmother. She's flying in from Indiana— her first time on an airplane. If I'm not there, she'll be frightened."

"I'm sorry, I wish I..." My tongue froze. *"Ye shall be witnesses."*... The words of the sermon rose above the wind and the waves.

Glancing over my shoulder at miles of shoreline, I opened my mouth and blurted, "Let me help you." *Why did I say that? I have to get my family checked out and on the road, too.*

"What does the key ring look like?" *What am I thinking?* Suddenly it dawned on me. I had prayed to the Lord for opportunities to witness, and maybe God was testing my sincerity. I was now committed.

"It's a round chrome thingy the keys fit on and…umm…a blue plastic triangle with a VW emblem. You're very kind, but this is my third trip up and down the beach. I guess I'll just have to fly back to meet my Grandma, get a locksmith for my apartment, and then fly back with the spare key to pick up my car."

I didn't want to fill her with false hope or cause her to miss a flight, but a powerful presence was driving me. "Tell you what, Miss…"

"Janet."

"Janet, you finish your search as far as you've been in that direction, and I'll trace back the other way to your hotel. It's worth one more shot with two pairs of eyes."

"Are you sure? I don't want to waste your time."

I nodded. "I'm sure." At that point I was very sure. What's more, I saw a touch of sun appearing between the clouds. Humans love signs, and this looked like one to me.

"My hotel is the tall, light-green one next to the boardwalk." She pointed it out, smiled weakly, and then continued her start, stop, stoop, and sift motions away from me.

Raising my face to the softening breeze, I silently prayed. *Lord, I know You're not in the business of recovering lost keys, but if You're giving me this chance to witness, then use me to help this girl.*

Before I opened my eyes, I heard a metallic tinkling—the sound of a ring full of keys being coaxed ashore by a dying wave. When I dared to look, reflections from the brass and silver ring sprinkled my shirt with light.

I stooped down and grasped a blue plastic triangle, embellished with a VW symbol. Suspended on the round chrome "thingy" were several keys waiting to be claimed by a young girl named Janet.

I held it high and waved it back and forth through narrow beams of sunlight. Now I was sobbing. I watched her suddenly stand to her feet and turn to me as if I had shouted her name, only I hadn't.

She ran. I ran. We met and cried in thankfulness together. Then we laughed.

"Are you some kind of angel?" Janet asked, her eyes searching my face.

"Not hardly, but I do know their Boss, and He occasionally sends an angel to help me out. My family and I are here for our annual church convention, and with so many believers in Pensacola, I know that God is walking among us."

"My grandmother belongs to that same church. She tried to get me to attend it with her, but I've been so busy. Maybe this small miracle with my keys is a wake-up call for me. Thank you again. I'll never forget what you've done for me."

"Don't thank me. I'm only His instrument." I pointed skyward. "However, you might take your grandmother up on her invitation when you see her. Then you can thank my angel's Boss in person."

She smiled as we shook hands, and with a wave, she sprinted back to her hotel.

I gazed up at the last gold-tinged clouds, still masking the sun.

"God, You have all the power to create a universe, to calm the seas, and to raise the dead. Yet You took the time to return a ring of keys. Just as I've witnessed to Janet, You've witnessed to me."

Twenty years have passed, and I still think about what Janet called "this small miracle with my keys." Her life may have been forever changed by this experience. And me? I know my faith and trust in the infinite mercy of the Father grew that morning. I often wonder: Did God send an angel to scoop a set of keys out of the ocean to drop them at my feet in answer to my ten-second prayer? To me, that is no small miracle.

God can use anything, even a childhood memory or the death of someone close, to remind us of where we should be headed. John found that out in a very profound way.

Getting Lost, Getting Home

BY NAN McKENZIE KOSOWAN, KITCHENER, ONTARIO, CANADA

My friend Joyce was full of that special kind of excitement that underlines her passion for neat endings, especially for lost souls who make successful U-turns in the direction of their lives.

"One of the best funerals I ever attended," she said brightly, clapping her hands together as though to catch and hold the memory, "was as much about a reclaimed life as about the death of our dear, wonderful friend Peter."

Of all the memories shared by family and friends at Peter's funeral service, one by the dead man's younger brother, John, affected Joyce the most. She knew that John had lived on the "wild side" of life. She had been praying that his big brother Peter's peace, Christian living, and the testimony of friends who spoke there that day would touch John. But it was John's testimony that affected them all.

When John's turn came to share something about Peter's life, he told of a bittersweet childhood experience in his homeland of Holland during the Second World War. Every week John and his big brother, Peter, would pull their sleds to the neighbor's farm over the fields and the frozen canal to get wood for cooking and heating. They always looked forward to going because the neighbor lady always gave them supper before they left for home.

On one of those trips, when John was nine years old, the boys got lost and wandered cold and crying, trying to get home through sudden, heavy fog. They trudged endlessly in circles until Peter said they should stop, fold their hands, bow their heads, and pray for God's help to find their way home. They did so, and then proceeded to wander for some time, not knowing where they were going until John burst out in exasperation and fear, "It doesn't work! Prayer doesn't work!"

Peter stopped and said, "Well, we'll do it again. God answers prayer." The two children prayed once more. At that moment, the sun broke through the fog. They saw where they were and headed gratefully for home.

"Sometimes we get lost in life, really lost," John told the mourners, most of whom knew that as a grown man John had strayed from the Lord for many years. "But two years ago, God spoke to my heart," he said, "reminding me of that time in Holland during the war when we were lost as kids. I stopped, folded my hands, bowed my head, and prayed for God's help to find my way home. I was praying the same prayer again. And God has answered my prayer again."

"That adventure in the fog when he was a little kid is more than just a cute story," said Joyce at the end of her story.

"Peter had given his little brother the keys to a safe return, and prayer got him back home to his loved ones not once, but twice! We can all hope someone will boast over us at our funerals someday like John boasted over his big brother, Peter, that day!"

> *"Point your kids in the right direction—when they're old they won't be lost"* (Proverbs 22:6 msg).

About the Contributors to God Answers Prayers

Candy Abbott, founder of Delmarva Christian Writers' Fellowship and published author, was named "Writer of the Year" at the 2003 Greater Philadelphia Christian Writers Conference. She and her husband, Drew, own and operate Fruit-Bearer Publishing. She may be reached at P.O. Box 777, Georgetown, DE 19947; or on-line at *candy.abbott@verizon.net* or *www.fruitbearer.com.*

Andrea Boeshaar is a bestselling, award-winning author of 17 novels, 8 novellas, and a host of articles and devotional stories. She and her husband, Daniel, live in southeastern Wisconsin. For more about Andrea, visit her Web site at *www.andrea boeshaar.com.*

Kevin Bottke has decided to keep his day job and not move to Pamplona, Spain, for the annual running of the bulls. You can reach him at *Kevin@godallowsuturns.com.*

Renie Burghardt, freelance writer, was born in Hungary. Her stories have appeared in many books and magazines including *God Allows U-Turns, Cup of Comfort* books, *Mature Living, Guideposts,* and others. She lives in the country and loves nature, animals, hiking, gardening, and spending time with family and friends.

R. T. Byrum is the author of eight Carver Cousins adventure books for young adults. He also writes radio and TV commercials, content books, magazine and e-zine articles, and serves as president of the Christian Authors Guild in Georgia. Visit Byrum's Web site at *www.rtbwriter.com.*

Penelope Carlevato, English-born, freelance writer, speaker, and registered nurse, has a passion for "Hospitali-tea" and is a popular speaker for women's retreats and events. Residing in Knoxville, Tennessee, she has eight grandchildren and is founder of PenelopesTeaTime.com and "Taste of Britain Tea Tours," Web site *PenelopesTeaTime.com,* phone: 865-310-7080.

Joan Clayton was named "Woman of the Year" for 2003 in her city. She has written 7 books, been included in 47 anthologies, and has over 450 articles published in various publications. She is religion columnist for her local newspaper. Her Web site is *www.joanclayton.com.*

Roger Allen Cook is a pastor and a Christian school administrator who is happily married and has four children and five grandchildren. His book *Sailing by Grace* has been well-received, and he has been published in many on-line magazines. Contact him at *rkcook@comcast.net*.

Mike Dandridge, author of two books, *The Divine Spark* and *Thinking Outside the Bulb*, is also an entertaining speaker. He and his wife, Frances, live in Temple, Texas, and lead the Bible study for adults at First Christian Church in Temple, Texas. You may visit Mike's Web site at *www.thedivinespark.com*.

P. Jeanne Davis is a homemaker and writer. Her work has appeared in *GRIT Magazine, The Lookout, Mothering, Chicken Soup for the Soul, Brave Hearts Magazine, Take a Break,* and *Woman Alive* (U.K.). She is a contributing writer at *Positively Woman*.

Wendy Dellinger lives in the beautiful foothills of the Colorado Rockies, enjoying the outdoors with her family. She spends her days as a wife and homeschooling mom, and writes to encourage others, especially women, in their journey of faith.

Iris Gray Dowling is a freelance writer from Cochranville, Pennsylvania, who writes church program materials, puppet skits, and stories. Her work is published in many collections by Standard Publishing and in *Bible Pathways for Children*. She has written five books of useful ideas for church workers.

T. Suzanne Eller is an author and international speaker. She and Richard just celebrated their twenty-fifth anniversary. To find out more about Suzie or her ministry to teens, go to *http://daretobelieve.org* or e-mail her at *tseller@daretobelieve.org*.

Susan Farr Fahncke is the author of *Angel's Legacy* and the coauthor of and contributor to numerous other books. Susan also runs Angels2TheHeart, a foundation that sends care packages and cards to critically ill people. She lives in Utah and teaches on-line writing workshops. Visit her Web site at *2TheHeart.com*.

Sharon Fawcett lives in Petitcodiac, New Brunswick, Canada, and is the mother of two teenage daughters. She and her husband, Tim, recently celebrated their twentieth wedding anniversary. Sharon enjoys volunteering at a local elementary school, serving in her church, writing, and singing. She is currently writing a book to bring hope to people with depression. Contact her by e-mail at *fawcettsharon@hotmail.com*.

Rusty Fischer is a full-time freelance writer who lives, writes, and works with his beautiful wife, Martha, in sunny Orlando, Florida. He first appeared in *God Allows U-Turns, Volume 3: A Woman's Journey*.

Susanna Flory is a freelance writer in Castro Valley, California. Married and a mother of two, she recently traveled to Cuba for a short-term missions project. "You haven't lived until you've worshiped with Cubans," she says. You can contact her at *irishbreakfast@comcast.net.*

Susan Foster serves as a ministering elder at Capistrano Community Church. She and her husband, Steve, reside in Laguna Niguel, California. They are the parents of two grown daughters.

Nancy B. Gibbs is the author of four books, a contributor to numerous anthologies and national magazines, a weekly religion columnist for two newspapers and a motivational speaker. Please visit her Web site at *www.nancybgibbs.com* or email her at *nancybgibbs@aol.com.*

Barbara E. Haley, published author of adult inspirational books, children's fiction, and devotional material, has worked as an elementary-school teacher, Sunday school teacher, Bible quiz coach, and private piano instructor. Barbara and her husband have three grown children and live near San Antonio, Texas.

Clement Hanson practices Occupational Medicine with Health One in Denver, Colorado. He and his wife, Mary, are active members of Denver's Montview Boulevard Presbyterian Church. You can contact Clem and Mary at *hanson139@comcast.net.*

Bob Haslam, a freelance writer, resides in Lynnwood, Washington. His articles have appeared in more than 60 Christian publications, plus five books. He has served as a pastor, missionary, missions executive, and magazine and book editor, and he mentors 50 students through the Jerry Jenkins Christian Writers Guild.

Sharon Hinck is a wife and mother of four with a master's degree in Communication from Regent University. When she is not writing, Sharon manages a direct-sales craft business and enjoys speaking to church groups. For an update on her current writing projects, visit *www.sharonhinck.com.*

B.J. Jensen is a talented speaker, author, and entertainer. Co-Founders of *CLR Ministries,* BJ and hubby Doug travel nationwide facilitating workshops and retreats for couples. Together the Jensens co-authored *Famous Lovers in the Bible and the Marriage Building Secrets We Learn From Their Relationships. www.CREATELOVINGRELATIONSHIPS.org*

Anne Johnson, is a wife, mother, freelance writer, and registered nurse. Her greatest joys in life are being a wife and mother; however, she has found that writing allows her to share her heart with more people, and through the stories she shares, she hopes to convey God's never-ending love.

Bob Kelly founded WordCrafters, Inc. in 1979, providing writing and editing services for speakers, ministries, and businesses. An award-winning author/coauthor of 16 books, he draws heavily on his quotation collection of 400 volumes and 1.5 million quotes. Contact him at (480) 895-7617 or *quotes@robsoncom.net*.

Sharon M. Knudson is a freelance writer and inspirational speaker. She is president of the Minnesota Christian Writers Guild *(www.mnchristianwriters.org)* and likes to teach writing classes. Sharon and her husband, Bob, are very active in their church and live in St. Paul, Minnesota.

Nan McKenzie Kosowan of Kitchener, Ontario, Canada, is fascinated at finding jewels of human nature in stories of real people that are funny, sad, heroic, or commonplace. It has kept her watching, listening, and writing to touch readers' hearts for over 50 years. Her website is *www.Dovenan.com.*

Dr. Muriel Larson, author of 17 books and more than 7500 first and reprint published writings and songs, is a professional Christian writer, speaker, and e-mail counselor for two on-line publications, and has taught at writers' conferences across the nation. You may contact her at *MKLJOY@aol.com.* For advice by e-mail, write her at *Doctormuriel@aol.com.*

Jan Roadarmel Ledford's latest novel, *The Cloning,* is featured at *www.biosocialethics.com.* Other writings include devotionals, poems, short stories, and 13 nonfiction books. She is an avid *The Lord of the Rings* fan. Jan lives in Franklin, North Carolina, and enjoys line dancing and playing with her cats.

Delores Liesner loves writing, speaking, and interviewing. She reveals dynamic hope and confidence found in the heavenly heritage of our personal God. Her best jewels are her husband, Ken, and family: Laurel, Doug, Aimee, Ben, Cheryl, Frank, Michael, Kristin, David, Daniel, Kimberly, Faith, Kevin, and Kris. Delores is a CLASS graduate. E-mail her at *lovedliftedandled@wi.rr.com.* Her Web site is *DeloresLiesner.com.*

Deanna Luke offers one message when speaking and writing: encouragement. She believes each person was born with a gift and, when operating in it, will find their joy. Values, integrity, and principles are central to her life. She teaches writing and publishing in many forums, including Barnes and Noble stores.

Lowell Lundstrom has been an evangelist/pastor for the past thirty-seven years. He served as president of Trinity Bible College in Ellendale, North Dakota, for seven years, been featured on his weekly radio and television programs for twenty-five years, written fifteen books, and recorded sixty music albums. Over 500,000 people have made decisions for Christ at his interdenominational crusades.

Emory May began writing while in junior high school. Upon graduation, he entered the ministry and has spent the past 47 years as a pastor, teacher, and missionary. He now lives in the Fiji Islands. He has written three novels, numerous children's stories, and inspirational articles.

Sandra McGarrity is the author of two Christian novels, *Woody* and *Caller's Spring*. Her writing has been published in volumes 3 and 4 of *God Allows U-Turns* and in many other publications. Visit her Web page at *www.heartwarmers4u.com/ members?woody*.

Jennifer McMahan is a wife, mother, and business owner who hopes to minister through her gifts of writing, speaking, and organizing, believing that committing each day to God is the most important aspect of organizing your life. Her Web site is *www.spacesimplicity.com*.

Cheryl Scott Norwood is wife of college sweetheart Mike Norwood, "mother" to Jazzy, our Siamese princess; full time paralegal, and part-time freelance writer. Co-founder of Cherokee Christian Writers Group (now the Christian Writers Guild); over 20 stories, articles and poems published in the past 4 years .

Ann Oliver lives in Tyler, Texas and enjoys writing for magazines. She has several stories published with Good Old Days magazine and is in two of their books. She feels she touches the lives of others with her stories.

Karen O'Connor is an award-winning author of more than 40 books, a popular speaker at women's events, a frequent guest on radio and television shows, and a writing mentor. In 2002 Karen received the Special Recognition Award at the Mount Hermon Christian Writers Conference.

Tom C. Rakow, D. Min., holds degrees from Bethel Theological Seminary, Asbury Theological Seminary, Moody Bible Institute, and the University of Wisconsin. He is a pastor and co-owner of Rock Dove Publications. Tom, his wife, Beth, and their four daughters reside in Minnesota. His Web site is *www.rockdove.com*.

Sandra Snider is a freelance writer with a journalism degree. Her writings have appeared in numerous local and national Christian and secular publications. She also contributes to *FaithWriters.com*, an on-line Web site for Christian writers.

Gloria Cassity Stargel, writer for *Guideposts* and other publications, urgently needed to know, "Does God still heal today?" The result is her award-winning book *The*

Healing, One Family's Victorious Struggle with Cancer. Read portions at *www.bright morning.com.* Order on-line at 1-800-888-9529; or write her at Applied Images, 312 Bradford Street NW, Gainesville, GA 30501.

Suzan Strader grew up in the church. She teaches Bible classes and speaks to groups in order to encourage listeners to become the persons God intended by trusting and obeying Jesus. Suzan has written articles for newsletters, magazines, and books.

Dennis Van Scoy Sr. was born and raised in Council Bluffs, Iowa. He retired from his police career for medical reasons in 1991. Dennis is now a freelance Christian writer, residing in Red Oak, Iowa, with his wife, Debbie, both serving Jesus Christ as Lord.

June L. Varnum is a published author of short stories and various magazine articles and devotions. She is an avid reader, amateur photographer, gardener, walks one or two miles on most days, and loves to share time and meals with family and friends and host tea parties.

Phyllis Wallace created and hosted the *Woman to Woman* radio show, which for 12 years and 1,200 shows, equipped women for "busy" boundaries, body, and beliefs with a biblically grounded perspective. A freelance writer, broadcaster, and retreat speaker, her insights energize and inspire women with the hope found in Christ.

Thelma Wells is an international inspirational speaker who shares heart-to-heart encouragement. She is a speaker at Women of Faith, president of A Woman of God Ministries, and Daughters of Zion Leadership Mentoring Program in Dallas, Texas, and a professor at Master's Divinity School, Evansville, Indiana. She is the author of *The Buzz* and *Bumblebees Fly Anyway.*

Reverend Michael F. Welmer is senior pastor of Epiphany Lutheran Church in Houston, Texas. He has been in the ministry for 31 years. Pastor Welmer received his master of divinity degree from Concordia Theological Seminary, Springfield, Illinois.

Lou Killian Zywicki is a freelance writer and a full-time teacher of college composition, literature, and business writing at the Secondary Technical Center in Duluth, Minnesota. The mother of four adult children, she lives in a rural nature paradise with her husband, Ernie.

About Our Editors

Allison Bottke is the Founder of the God Allows U-Turns Project, and lead editor in all the books developed under this popular umbrella brand. Allison frequently speaks at women's events and writing conferences around the country. Visit her Web site for more information on Allison and the exciting u-turns outreach. *www.godallowsuturns.com*

Cheryll M. Hutchings is co-editor and administrative assistant of the popular God Allows U-Turns Project, an international outreach ministry founded by Allison Bottke.

A Christian since the age of 12, Cheryll has always let God lead her in life. The best adventure He's lead her on so far has been joining the God Allows U-Turns Project on the ground floor of the ministry when it began in 2000. Reading countless stories submitted by contributing authors from around the world, Cheryll was instrumental in the development and editing of the first four books in the God Allows U-Turns series, as well as the most recent books in the new God Answers Prayers series. Married to Bob for 27 years, they have a 22-year-old son Aaron, who is working full time in the computer industry, and a 19-year-old son Scott, who is a Corporal in the Marine Corps. They live in the country on a rambling ranch in Medina, Ohio, sitting in several acres of peaceful seclusion, surround by the Lord's beautiful nature and wildlife.

Sharen Watson resides in Spring, TX (with Denver, CO fast approaching) with Ray, her college sweetheart and "most supportive" husband of 24 years. They have a married daughter, one son in college, another son in high school and one spoiled Lhasa Apso. Sharen is Founder/Director of Words for the Journey Christian Writer's Guild. She also leads women's Bible studies and speaks her testimony of God's enduring faithfulness and love. Her desire is that every word she speaks and writes will be a reflection of God's hope, restoration, and joy. You can visit her Web site at *www.WordsfortheJourney.org*

10 Tips on How to Pray

1. Set aside a short time each day to meet with God. Yes, God hears our short "bullet prayers" throughout the day, but true fellowship wants more than that. Keep your appointment with God, just as you would any other appointment. Start by making these divine encounters brief. Even five minutes a day is a great start. You can add more time once the habit is established.

2. If you feel awkward at first, or your mind wanders, or you get a bit sleepy, do not feel guilty. God understands. Take a moment to read a few verses from Psalms or the day's entry in your favorite daily devotional book. It may take time to get used to being in the presence of God.

3. Ask God to help you pray. Prayer, after all, is His invention. He designed prayer as the means for us to communicate with Him. Let Him be your Teacher.

4. One very good place to start praying is to simply confess any known sin to God and claim His forgiveness. At this same time, be sure you harbor no bitterness toward anyone else. Unforgiveness can hinder your prayers. If a specific person with whom you have hard feelings comes to mind, ask God to forgive you and change your heart. If necessary, go to the other person and make things right.

5. Remember, prayer is more than asking for things. God loves it when we just take time to praise Him for who He is and thank Him for the blessings He has given us.

219

6. If you are likely to forget what you want to pray about, start a small written prayer list where you jot down the things you want to pray for.

7. Some people find it useful to actually write out their prayers and keep a journal of when and how God answers. For other people, a journal may seem a distraction. Try it and see if it works for you.

8. Look for other opportunities to pray throughout the day. Waiting in line at the supermarket, washing the dishes, sitting in traffic…these are all excellent times to talk to God.

9. Remember the stories in chapter 10 when people asked God to use them to touch another life. Ask God to do the same through you. Then watch for the divine appointments He will set up throughout the day.

10. Above all, consider your time with God a call to *joy*, not some staid, dry religious exercise. Learn to delight in God as you pray. He delights in you!

About the God Allows U-Turns Project®

ALONG WITH THESE EXCITING new Answered Prayer books published by Harvest House, we want to share with readers the entire scope of the powerful God Allows U-Turns outreach of hope and healing.

The broad outreach of this organization includes the book you now hold in your hands, as well as other nonfiction and fiction books for adults, youth, and children. Written by Allison Gappa Bottke along with other collaborating authors and coeditors, there are currently 14 books available under the God Allows U-Turns umbrella brand, with 5 additional books releasing in 2005 and 2006, including Allison's first novel in the "chick-lit" genre.

More than 50,000 copies of the God Allows U-Turns tract, featuring Allison's powerful testimony of making a U-turn toward God, have been distributed around the world.

There is a line of nine God Allows U-Turns greeting cards touching on difficult times when new direction is needed. Also available is an entire line of merchandise featuring the highly recognizable God Allows U-Turns signature yellow road sign, items such as Bible book covers, ball caps, and such. Also in development is a God Allows U-Turns TV interview talk show and a national speakers tour.

Sharing the life-saving message that you can never be so lost or so broken that you cannot turn toward God is Allison's main passion in her life and in her ministry.

Visit your local bookstore or the God Allows U-Turns Web site (*www.godallowsuturns.com*) to find out more about this exciting ministry that is helping to change lives, or write:

Allison Bottke
The God Allows U-Turns Project
P.O. Box 717
Faribault, MN 55021-0717

editor@godallowsuturns.com

The God Allows U-Turns Foundation®

One of the most profound lessons in the Bible is that of giving. The Holy Bible is quite clear in teaching us how we are to live our lives. Scripture refers to this often, and never has the need to share with other people been so great.

"Give, and it will be given to you. A good measure, pressed down, shaken together and running over, will be poured into your lap. For with the measure you use, it will be measured to you" (Luke 6:38).

In keeping with the lessons taught us by the Lord our God, we are pleased to have the opportunity to donate a portion of the net profits of every God Allows U-Turns book to one or more nonprofit Christian charities. These donations are made through the God Allows U-Turns Foundation, a funding mechanism established by Kevin and Allison Bottke as a way to share the success of the growing U-Turns outreach ministry.

For more details visit the Web site at
www.godallowsuturns.com.

God Answers Prayers

Submit Your True Story!

The stories you have read in this volume were submitted by readers just like you. From the very start of this inspiring and compelling book series, it has been our goal to encourage people from around the world to submit for publication their slice-of-life, true short stories of how God answers prayers.

Please visit the God Allows U-Turns Web site at *www.godallowsuturns.com* for information on upcoming volumes in development, as well as for writer's guidelines and deadlines.